CUBS WIN!

A CELEBRATION OF THE 1984 CHICAGO CUBS

BY BOB LOGAN

CONTEMPORARY
BOOKS, INC.
CHICAGO

All photos courtesy of the *Chicago Tribune* and Chicago Cubs. Cover photos and photo of Jim Frey and Bob Logan by Stephen Green. The author thanks Andy McKenna, Jim Finks, Dallas Green, and the Cubs' organization for their assistance.

Published by Contemporary Books, Inc.
180 North Michigan Avenue, Chicago, Illinois 60601
Manufactured in the United States of America
International Standard Book Number: 0-8092-5299-6

Published simultaneously in Canada by Beaverbooks, Ltd.
195 Allstate Parkway, Valleywood Business Park
Markham, Ontario L3R 4T8 Canada

This book is for Jack Brickhouse,
a winner, even when the Cubs were losing.

BOB LOGAN
Chicago, 1984

CONTENTS

FOREWORD

Cubs Win! That's sure the right title for this book. I don't know anybody who could write about this exciting, spine-tingling chapter of Chicago baseball history better than Bob Logan, a real pro from the *Tribune*.

Following the Cubs on every step of their road to the top has been a terrific adventure for me and all of you Cub fans. Now here's a chance to relive an action-packed season.

Holy Cow! Fans, I guarantee you'll love this success story. It's an up-close look at the 1984 Cubs from Dallas Green's planning to Rick Sutcliffe's pitching. Enjoy.

Harry Caray

Here it is, in all its No-Lights splendor. Wrigley Field, built for the Chicago Whales, has been the focal point of Cub Mania since 1916.

Harry Caray isn't cowed by some ribbing of his "Holy Cow!" trademark.

1
"LEMME HEAR YA, CUB FANS!"

CUB FEVER.

It's Wrigley Field dissolving into bedlam when Harry Caray leans out of his WGN-TV broadcasting booth during the seventh-inning stretch to bellow:

"Awww-right! Lemme REALLY hear ya, Cub fans."

It's no more suffering for the rooters packed into the North Side baseball museum that no longer is a mausoleum.

It's cards, letters, phone calls, telegrams from everywhere under the sun, pouring into Chicago's patch of endless sunshine. They arrive from Moose Jaw, Saskatchewan, from Vera Cruz, Mexico, and all points east, west, north, or south. Everybody wants a ticket, an autographed picture, or just an affirmation that this really is happening, that the Cubs are no mirage.

It's store marquees all over Chicago sporting signs reading "Cubs—7 ahead, 20 to play" instead of "Rutabaga special, $1.98."

It's President Reagan, who recreated Cub games in 1935 on radio station WHO in Des Moines, declaring in 1984, "The miracle is happening at last. The Cubs are on their way to the National League pennant." It's also press secretary Jim Brady, who knows a miracle when he sees one, flashing the Cubs a "V" for victory sign.

Cub fans get goggle-eyed with glee when Wrigley Field favorite Leon "Bull" Durham comes over to sign pregame autographs.

Harry Caray changes caps in 1981.

Steve "Rainbow" Trout finds a home in Wrigley Field after being unloaded by the White Sox. Cub fans appreciate the left-hander, especially the way he's pitched this season.

It's people turning off daytime soap operas all over America when the real-life adventures of the Cubs appear on their television screens.

It's Cub first baseman Leon Durham giving Chicago public schools $750 every time he hits a Wrigley Field homer, so that kids can play games instead of getting into trouble.

It's a trickle of hardy types arriving in early-morning darkness to huddle near gate "N" at Waveland and Sheffield, growing to a throng before the bleacher ticket windows open on game mornings.

It's a capacity crowd of 37,275 sitting, and a few thousand more standing in every Wrigley Field nook and cranny, loaded down with Cub caps, T-shirts, pennants, and assorted souvenirs. They'll drink about 100,000 cups of cold drinks during the game, with beer a 2-to-1 favorite over soda, washing down tons of hot dogs, pizza, nachos, peanuts, and candy. Despite a noisy afternoon exhorting the Cubs, the fans have plenty of energy left to sing along with maestro Caray, leading them in "Take Me Out to the Ball Game." The all-time attendance record of 1,674,993, set in (gulp!) 1969, toppled on

August 28. The Cubs will top 2 million at home for the only time in their 109 NL seasons. A Cub ticket now conveys clout in Chicago.

It's the Chicago Cubs, thumbing their noses at the TV networks' greed and ending a 39-year famine by winning in daylight.

It's Steve Stone, Milo Hamilton, and Lou Boudreau in the broadcast booth with Harry, keeping fans both informed and entertained with the inside scoop on what's happening on the field.

Most of all, it's fun. To their surprise, Chicagoans discovered that just about everybody around the nation who is served by cable television also loves the Cubs. Some are of the jump-on-the-bandwagon variety, anxious to identify with this year's "in" team. Others are lifelong fans who suffered with a mediocre team for decades. They all got caught up in the 1984 blend of excitement, emotion, and victory.

NATIONWIDE FANATICISM

The response is astonishing. Wherever the Cubs go, their legions show up, waving hand-lettered signs urging them on to their first National League Eastern Division championship. Even Caray, in the broadcasting business for 41 years, can't recall the entire nation going this ga-ga over one baseball team.

"It's remarkable," Caray said. "When we were in Houston, about three-quarters of the crowd had Cub banners. People in remote areas can't come to Chicago, because it's too far away. So they pick out the nearest city, Cincinnati, Pittsburgh, Houston, San Diego, or wherever, look up the schedule to see when the Cubs will be there, and plan the trip. In Montreal, people from upstate New York were there to root for the Cubs.

"I've never seen anything like it. Fans keep sending up cards and notes to the booth. If we read them all on the air, I wouldn't have time to broadcast the game."

Harry's son, Skip Caray, saw something akin to this happening to the Atlanta Braves before the Cubs swiped their act. He telecasts games on Ted Turner's Atlanta superstation, WTBS, where the Braves bill themselves as "America's Team," with no apologies to the Dallas Cowboys.

"A lot of people adopted the Braves, because we got to the nationwide audience first," Skip said. Harry agreed, but pointed out that things have changed this season.

"The Cub fans have been waiting so long for a contender, they're going wild," he said. "And their games on cable create new fans every day."

Despite that, WGN-TV is shut out of playoff and World Series action under the exclusive network agreement with baseball. Caray's trademark, "Holy Cow!," will be confined to radio in the post-season.

THIS TIME, IT'S FOR REAL

It took time for wary Chicagoans to be convinced the Cubs were real, especially those with long memories of the great foldup of 1969. But fear struck out when the 1984 Cubs beat the New York Mets seven straight times, capping a blistering streak that caused a 12-game swing in NL East standings. They took the NL East lead for keeps on August 1, and Cub Fever became an incurable disease. The Emil Verban Memorial Society and other old-line boosters joined forces with new groups like the Diehard Fan Club in a stampede to

Security guards restrain the Mets' coach Bill Robinson from jumping into the stands to tangle with hecklers. Tempers flared when batters were dusted off in a crucial Mets-Cubs series.

This is the way it was before the Cubs lit up Chicago in 1984. Rick Reuschel pitches in near empty Wrigley Field, with a crowd of 2,092 in May 1981, watching the Cubs lose to the Astros.

the box office or the nearest radio or TV set.

Only Steve Dahl, running amok in a disco, could shatter more records than the 1984 Cubs. Since June 1, their record is the best in baseball. They eat up left-handed pitchers, carve out a winning record on the road, even on artificial turf, lead the league in RBI, and set a ton of personal bests.

By no coincidence, the surge coincided with the arrival of Rick Sutcliffe, a genial 6'7" giant, whose strawberry-colored beard promptly earned him the label of "the Red Baron." It proved accurate, as well as colorful, because Baron von Sutcliffe shot down NL batters while the Cubs shot upward in the standings.

Sutcliffe's pitching exploits were the big story, especially the right-hander's 4–0 shutout of the Mets on September 8 before a hostile Shea Stadium throng. It would have been impossible to top the one-hit, 10–0 coat of whitewash slapped on the Cubs by teen-aged titan Dwight Gooden in the series opener, but Sutcliffe came close. More important, he made sure younger Cubs wouldn't panic in the heat of their first pennant race.

The Red Baron's 12-strikeout show probably ranked as the Cubs' most important victory of the regular season. It wasn't unprecedented, because the Cubs already had learned how to deal with adversity, earning the title "Cardiac Cubs" for their

finesse at pulling thrillers out of the fire. The team believed in itself long before the fans did. Cub teams have had a tradition of blowing close games, from those 12–11 Wrigley Field demolition derbies, when the wind blew out and baseballs flew out, to the standard 2–1 morale crushers. Not the 1984 Cubs.

They started winning the squeakers, and kept right on doing so. Finally, there was enough ability on hand to turn the tide, but the men who landed the right players and inserted them in the right spots were general manager Dallas Green and manager Jim Frey.

"I'm a big believer in approach, attitude, and chemistry of the 25 guys on the roster" Green said. "If you can light that fire and keep it going by replacing deadheads with talent, you're heading in the right direction. I was convinced the Cubs were at that point in spring training, although nobody in Chicago believed me."

There was ample reason for skepticism when the 1984 Cubs assembled in Mesa, Arizona. It looked like the customary June swoon had been accelerated by three months, because an 11-game losing streak dropped their exhibition mark to 3–18, the worst in Arizona, Florida, or anywhere in between. Green and Frey were worried, though not by the record or the suspicion that the Cubs might really be that bad.

"I was very troubled," Green confessed. "You don't win the pennant in the Cactus League or the Grapefruit League, but we had guys in the outfield dropping balls that should have been caught. Others were so sure of their jobs, they didn't have any oomph or enthusiasm.

"Self-satisfaction can destroy ability, and a lot of teams don't wake up from being satisfied."

Well, the Cubs woke up, as the sporting world knows by now. How it happened and who did it are subjects that will warm cold Chicago winters and enliven baseball bull sessions for years to come.

There was some frustration and disappointment along the way, though surprisingly little. For the most part, the Cubs' turnaround was an upbeat story, one that captured the country's imagination. Americans enjoy cheering for the reformed wimp who springs to life and kicks the bully right in the standings.

And that's what happened in Chicago. The Cubs whacked the daylights—no pun intended—out of unsuspecting visitors.

"The Cubs don't just beat you here; they blow you out," lamented Houston's Terry Puhl after the Astros had been mugged 11–5. "They punish you."

Green had vowed those bad old days were over. Puhl was admitting that the man was right.

NO LIGHTS IN WRIGLEY FIELD

Not even the uproar over heavy-handed attempts to impose lights for night baseball on Wrigley Field could detract from the Cub victory march. At its best, television can do a lot of good for baseball, such as spreading Cub Fever to cable viewers. At its worst, television can and will sap the vitality from a sport and then discard it, like roller derby or boxing.

The Cubs, who've played in the NL since General Custer was alive, even before the first beer commercial appeared, were "punished" by the TV networks and their allies in the commissioner's office. They stripped the Cubs of their home-field advantage for the crime of playing in daylight, awarding the odd game of each series to the opposing team's park. The only comic relief in the affair was a bleat by ABC and NBC that "no pressure" had been applied to insure night games and maxi-profits.

At least the episode proved the mettle of Cubs'

president Jim Finks, who had been looked on with suspicion by some fans because his background was in football, as general manager of the Chicago Bears and Minnesota Vikings. Finks handled the network and baseball moguls with diplomacy and tact, working out an acceptable compromise for the Cubs. Until then, Wrigley Field neighborhood groups had threatened court action to enforce city and state laws restricting noise pollution in the area after 10 P.M.

Everybody was relieved to get back to baseball, even though Green, Frey, and many fans were disgusted by the new arrangement that forced the Cubs to play more road games in postseason action.

"If we had played at night, the whole atmosphere of Wrigley Field would have been changed," Finks summed up.

But Cub fans were no longer in the dark about their team's ability. The only remaining question was how high the hysteria index would climb before they took the field for their first-ever playoff game. Incredibly, it was the first time the Cubs had won anything since losing the 1945 World Series to the Detroit Tigers. As the division title came closer to reality, voices from the past were heard, not to bring back haunting memories of the 1969 collapse, but to join in the celebration.

"This Cub team knows how to win," said Ernie Banks, the beloved Mr. Cub ("Let's play two today!"), whose retired No. 14 flaps in the breeze from a Wrigley Field flagpole. "All I want is a couple of tickets."

Jack Brickhouse, who saluted Cub homers with his "Hey! Hey!" trademark for 34 years of play-by-play on WGN, has one goal left in sports. "I want to see a Cub-White Sox World Series," Brick said. "The only time it happened, in 1906, President Reagan hadn't even been born."

But this is 1984, and the word from the TV booth is "Holy Cow!" It was first employed in the 1940s by young radio announcer Harry Caray, "so I wouldn't say something unprintable on the air by accident." He carried his pet phrase with him to Wrigley Field in '82, after spending eleven years in Comiskey Park doing White Sox games. Now 64, Caray has the same enthusiasm for baseball that carried him through a quarter-century as the voice of the St. Louis Cards.

This year, like all Cub fans, Harry has a lot more to be enthusiastic about.

2
"HERE COMES BABY RUTH"

For Cub fans, it was SOS—Same Old Suffering. Their heroes were losing another Wrigley Field slugfest, this time to the St. Louis Cards. The Cubs quickly fell behind 7–1 and still trailed 9–3 in the sixth inning. Nothing in this dreary scenario even hinted that June 23, 1984, would be the day Cub diehards had been pining for through 39 years of National League futility. Until Ryne Sandberg convinced them, a fourth generation of true believers was prepared for another ride on the same emotional roller coaster with a Cub team that started most seasons by raising their spirits and finished by breaking their hearts.

With dramatic home runs in consecutive trips to the plate, Sandberg changed all that. Instead of witnessing another defeat, the throng of 38,079 packing the North Side playpen that sunny Saturday afternoon became disciples of Cub victory mania. Suddenly, all the frustration of all those losing years belonged to a bygone era now known as BS—Before Sandberg. When his bat boomed twice, it touched off a wave of hysteria that soon spilled past Chicago's borders to exiled Cub fans all over America. Millions of viewers who caught the magic act on NBC's Game of the Week also caught Cub Fever, jumping on the bandwagon.

Ryne Sandberg: MVP-to-be.

Sandberg's first homer off St. Louis relief ace Bruce Sutter tied the game at 9–9 in the ninth inning. Gloom returned when the visitors pummeled Lee Smith for two runs in their half of the tenth. Sutter got the next two Cub batters, so only

Ken Oberkfell of the Braves is a dead duck at second, with Sandberg ready to nail him.

7

Sandberg gets the glad hand from third-base coach Don Zimmer after a ninth-inning homer off the Cards' Bruce Sutter.

a miracle could save them. Maybe that big Manager up in the sky let miracle worker Sandberg get another chance, because Bob Dernier coaxed a walk, bringing Ryno back to the batters' box.

Whitey Herzog, the astute Cards' manager, had a clear idea that a juggernaut was stirring. "Uh-oh," Herzog muttered to himself. "Here comes Baby Ruth."

Hollywood scriptwriters would have been fired for trying to convince movie moguls that Sandberg actually hit another game-tying homer in this spot. Regardless, when they film *The Ryne Sandberg Story* a few years from now, that's exactly what will happen. After reliable Ryne's one-two punch into the left-field bleachers, there was no stopping the Cubs. Rookie Dave Owen brought them home that day 12–11 with a bases-loaded single in the 11th inning, but the impact of Sandberg's back-to-back homers, five hits in six trips, and seven runs batted in—all in a single game—was staggering. No longer was it traditional for the Cubs to lose these wild games, as they did the 23–22 Wrigley Field classic taken by the Phillies on May 17, 1979.

"I'm in a state of shock," Sandberg confessed after that pivotal game. "I don't even know what day it is."

Cub fans now know it as the day the Cubs grew up. The big finish capped a three-game Sandberg spree of 12-for-16—a .750 clip—three homers and

eight RBI. Herzog couldn't conceal his awe. "Ryne Sandberg is the best player I ever saw," the Cards' skipper said. "I don't think anybody ever hit two home runs off Sutter in one game."

Sandberg became the symbol of overnight Cub transformation from clods to contenders. The soft-spoken second baseman made it happen, the same way he made everything else fall into place for the 1984 Cubs. Leadoff man Dernier and number 2 hitter Sandberg—the Daily Double—were the best baserunning and stealing duo since Bert Campaneris and Bill North of the mid-seventies Oakland A's dynasty. With Sandberg's scorching bat and golden glove as the catalyst, the Cubs played come-from-behind, even on the road, to grab first place in the National League East.

Dallas Green, the Cubs' general manager who had pirated Sandberg from Philadelphia, tempered Herzog's praise for Sandberg in a bid to take some pressure off the All-Star second baseman. The national media had belatedly discovered Sandberg and tried to embroil him in a feud with the Mets' Keith Hernandez over Most Valuable Player laurels, so Green's appraisal was a smart move: "That's probably stretching it," he said. "Ryne may not be the best player in the National League, but he ranks with the most consistent. Look at his contribution on defense, as a team player, giving himself up to move runners along, plus speed, pow-

Poetry in motion at second base: Sandberg robs another enemy batter with a diving grab.

er, and base stealing, and you have as consistent a player as we've seen in a long time."

TOO GOOD TO BE TRUE?

Coming into his third season with the Cubs in 1984, Sandberg was rewarded with a six-year contract worth almost $4 million, including incentive bonuses. Such honors as All-Star selection, MVP and Golden Glove awards, plus performance totals, could add to the jackpot. Sandberg's figures in 1,274 previous NL at-bats hinted at his enormous potential, and the 25-year-old sensation's fielding credentials are unimpeachable. Despite being moved from third base to second late in 1982, Sandberg last season became the first Cub to earn a Golden Glove since Don Kessinger in 1970. He led NL second sackers in fielding with a .986 percentage, making only 13 errors in 914 total chances. Early this season, he had a 38-game errorless streak, following it with a string of 47 straight. That one was broken by Atlanta's Claudell Washington, credited with an infield single on a tough call against Sandberg. Then, a late-season string of 61 flawless outings came to an end when he muffed a throw on September 7, in New York.

"I guess you get spoiled by the way Ryno eats up everything hit to him," shrugged Cubs' manager Jim Frey. "He's the best second baseman I've ever seen. I used to think Bobby Grich was, but now I have to say it's Sandberg. . . . This young man is so good, it's hard to put limits on what he can do."

Trite as it sounds, Ryne Dee Sandberg *is* almost

One of baseball's rare feats: Sandberg steals home, sliding past the tag of Padres' catcher Terry Kennedy.

too good to be true, both personally and professionally. The sturdy 6'2", 185 pounder is to the 1984 Cubs what slugger Ron Kittle was to the 1983 White Sox—an All-American image. Sandberg's quiet reserve contrasts sharply with the gregarious Kittle's one-liners, but they are mirror images in one vital category. Both are real people, devoid of the ego, strutting, and posturing displayed by players with far less talent. "Ryne is a genuinely polite and respectful person who looks up to the veteran ballplayers," Frey noted. "Some of them are starting to look up to him, but he hasn't changed."

Green was banking on Sandberg's character when he made him a millionaire with the long-term contract. Such instant riches have ruined a lot of promising players, replacing their hunger with fat-cat lethargy. Green is confident that will not happen to Sandberg. "I didn't have any qualms about Ryne's contract," the Cubs boss said. "I knew he'd give us the same kind of production he would with a one-year deal. He's just such a super kid.

"The recognition he's getting now is great, because he can handle it," Green pointed out. "Ryne is what you would hope all baseball players turn out to be. Even if he doesn't have the gung-ho of a Pete Rose, the same kind of inward drive is there. Sandberg has to play every game as tough as he can."

True. Teddy Roosevelt's advice about speaking softly and carrying a big stick is a way of life for Sandberg, who went the Rough Rider of San Juan Hill one better, adding a vacuum-cleaner glove as standard equipment. Along with all that ability, the Cubs' main man has inner stability to keep him cool when things heat up on the field. "I'm amazed to see the way such a young player handles himself in tough situations," said shortstop Larry Bowa, himself a fierce competitor. "Ryne's attitude is amazing."

Like his talent, Sandberg's low-key approach is simply based on doing what comes naturally. "That's just the way I am," he said. "If I stay on an even keel when clutch situations come up, it's easier to relax and do the job. That doesn't mean I'm not emotionally involved. On the field, I'm not that quiet. I know how to yell. When I played football in high school, I'd holler at guys and push them around when they got out of line."

That was during Sandberg's short-lived career as a quarterback in Spokane, Washington, proving to his satisfaction that he could take charge in the clutch. Even though he also lettered in basketball and football, baseball was the strong youngster's best game; he soon learned that his bat and glove could make more than enough noise on the diamond.

Sandberg still is not a holler guy in the Cubs' clubhouse, leaving that role to the right man, Gary "Sarge" Matthews. When Sandberg explains his emergence as the balance wheel of the NL's Cinderella team, the second baseman sticks to an honest appraisal. "Going out there with the same attitude and willingness to play hard every day is the key to consistency," Sandberg said of the 1984 campaign that shows many peaks, but few valleys, for him. "I think about ways to improve and make the plays better, even though everything seems easier and more fun when you're winning."

The Cubs struggled through 73–89 and 71–91 washouts in Sandberg's first two Chicago seasons. He knew things would be better this time, though frankly admitting that the Cubs' challenge for the NL East crown was "maybe a year ahead of schedule."

"Getting pitchers like Dennis Eckersley, Rick Sutcliffe, and George Frazier made us a much stronger club in the second half," he said. "With them and the way we kept playing well when guys were getting hurt, it gives us a positive feeling going down the stretch. We've learned how to play through adversity. Jim (Frey) kept bringing new people off the bench when starters got hurt and they came through for us."

The one time the Cubs wouldn't have been able to survive an injury provided their scariest moment of the season. Brimming with confidence after a four-game Wrigley Field sweep of the Mets, the Cubs stormed into the Houston Astrodome, a long-time Cub graveyard, on August 13 and almost saw their pennant hopes buried. Running out a grounder, Sandberg was blind-sided by first baseman Enos Cabell's knee when Cabell leaped for an errant throw. Sandberg crashed to the artificial turf and lay still while concerned teammates gathered around, their glances trading an unspoken plea: "Oh, no! Not Ryno!"

Providentially, Cabell's knee had bruised Sandberg's hip instead of cracking some ribs, so a sore

Ron Gardenhire of the Mets makes Sandberg take the high road on a successful theft of second base.

Sandberg only rested a few days before returning to action. Although he admitted to fatigue, the MVP candidate refused to ask for a breather. He was back in action on August 17, in time to battle Pete Rose's emotional return to Cincinnati as the player-manager.

Even though his power tapered off somewhat during the dog days of August, Sandberg kept clicking on all cylinders with key hits, stolen bases, and the customary carpet-sweeper defense. He believes that learning to go with the pitch has had a lot to do with his admission to the select company of .300 hitters. "I just try to drive the ball to all fields and be aggressive at the plate," Sandberg said. "I haven't done anything differently, like changing my swing or speeding it up."

Whatever he's doing, Sandberg is stylish. Rapidly becoming the premier keystone sacker in the NL, if not in both leagues, he should keep improving before reaching his peak four or five years down the road. By then, the family mantle in Tempe, Arizona, should be overloaded with MVP trophies and assorted hardware doled out annually at Hot Stove League banquets and other off-season affairs.

A REAL STEAL!

So the question resurfaces for the thousandth time since the Phillies foolishly let Sandberg slip

Frightening moment for Cub fans: Sandberg's down in the Astrodome after a collision at first base. Trainer Tony Garafolo tends to him while manager Jim Frey, umpire Randy Marsh, and coaches Ruben Amaro and John Vukovich watch.

through their fingers: How could they commit such a blunder in player evaluation? Sandberg is neither a free agent nor greedy, but if he were both, his agent could ring up astronomical numbers on a contract from the Yankees' George Steinbrenner or some other well-heeled owner.

Crafty Dallas Green deserves much credit for prying Sandberg loose (see the full story in the following chapter), but there's still plenty of blame to spread around the Philadelphia front office. The designated scapegoat turned out to be Bobby Wine, a loyal Phillies man for 23 years. His scouting report on Sandberg downgraded the young shortstop's chances to make it in the majors. "I said I didn't think he could equal a quality shortstop like Larry Bowa," Wine defended his judgment. "I also said he would be a good offensive player. It's unfair to blame me three years later because Sandberg turned out to be terrific."

The delicious irony for Cub fans is that the Phils traded Sandberg to Chicago on January 27, 1982, along with Bowa, the shortstop he wasn't supposed to compare with. He has played a grand total of

one inning at shortstop since becoming a Cub and now you couldn't get him for any shortstop, or almost any other player, in either league.

"This year, Sandberg's the most dominating player in the National League," asserted Paul Owens, the Phillies' manager. "Instead of trying to go the opposite way with every pitch, he's taken Jim Frey's advice, opened up his stance, and hit for power. "Now you can't jam him inside anymore," Owens added. "We sure made a mistake letting him go."

While serving as a Mets coach last season, Frey noticed that Sandberg often reacted like a slap hitter. "I saw a big kid with a great swing, trying to hit everything up the middle," Frey recalled. "He thought of himself as a guy who should advance runners. First time we got together in spring training, I told him I thought he was better than that." Obviously, Frey was right. The one-time singles hitter has become a threat to take pitchers downtown in game-breaking situations, the way Sandberg did to Sutter in June, the Dodgers' Tom Niedenfuer in July and the Braves' Rick Camp in August.

THE ALL-AMERICAN BOY

Making the right move has become a habit for the youngster, and he credits his parents, Derwent and Elizabeth Sandberg, with steering him in the right direction. Sandberg was destined to follow baseball, although the versatile athlete chose a football scholarship to Washington State University over baseball, until the Phillies tossed a $30,000 signing bonus at him in 1978. His dad named him after Ryne Duren, a fireballing Yankee relief pitcher of the fifties and sixties. Another Sandberg son, Del, was named for Del Ennis, left fielder of the Phillies' 1950 Whiz Kids. Nobody, suspected that Sandberg would eventually eclipse all of them.

Just like All-American boys should, Sandberg married his high school sweetheart, Cindy White, from Spokane's North Central High School. Daughter Lindsey was born in his rookie Cub season, and the day after Sandberg got his first Golden Glove award on May 5, 1984, Cindy presented him with a much bigger gift, son Justin.

"Cindy has been through it all with me in the minors," Sandberg said. "Now with a contract that gives us security, we can relax and enjoy our growing family, but I'll never forget how hard I had to work to get here.

"I was lucky to come to the Cubs when Dallas Green made the trade with Philadelphia," Sandberg reflected. "The timing was perfect, because I got a chance to play right away. The Phillies were loaded with guys like Bowa, Mike Schmidt, and Manny Trillo, so I'd probably still be a backup for them."

Not anymore—though with the way Sandberg started off at third base in 1982, it didn't look like the rookie could survive as a caddy for the unlamented Joe Strain, the Cub second baseman who Sandberg eventually replaced. Still adjusting to a new position, the anxious kid went 0-for-23 and 1-for-31 before his natural ability took over. "Lee Elia [fired as Cubs' manager on August 22, 1983] stuck with me," Sandberg related. "Nobody panicked, because I had shown in spring training that I could hit big-league pitching. It wouldn't have helped anybody to bench me. I was concentrating too much on making every play at third base, so when I stopped trying to swing too hard and hit everything out of the park, hits began to fall in."

Result?

"Instant superstar," said Cubs broadcaster Lou Boudreau. "Who can do all the things Sandberg does so well?"

Cub fans have a one-word answer: Nobody.

Sandberg looks for more action after tagging out the Phillies' Jeff Von Hayes.

3
GREEN LIGHT FOR RED-HOT CUBS

Just call him "Rocky."

Like Rocky Balboa I, II, and III, Dallas Green is a Philadelphia fighter. Rocky Green also won his first heavyweight title in the City of Brotherly Love, managing the Phillies to the 1980 world championship after building them into a contender on the front-office level. Then he came to Chicago, where things *really* got rocky.

A ROCKY START

The Cubs certainly were on the rocks when Green was unveiled as executive vice president and general manager, just after the 1981 season ended. The Tribune Co. had snapped up the Cubs a few months earlier for a bargain-basement $23 million, including real estate and $2.6 million in liabilities. The basement was the right place for the new owners to find a club chock-full of liabilities, most of them wearing Cub uniforms.

Change was badly needed, and Green was ready to bring that commodity to the Cubs when he was lured from Philadelphia by a five-year contract worth over $1 million. He was ready for controversy. "I won't back away from a fight," Green promised in his opening press conference, and he lived up to his word.

The press was critical, and many of Green's attempts to explain himself and his methods were greeted with skepticism, ridicule, or both. Green said, for instance, "When other baseball guys are home, working on their second martini, I'll still be at the office working. Anybody who works for me had better look at it the same way." The predictable media reaction: "We've heard all this big talk before."

So there was an early communications gap between the man from Philadelphia and the media people conveying his image to Chicago fans. And the gap would grow a lot wider before Green would vindicate himself with the 1984 Cubs. Tact never was Green's long suit, and he initially tried to get too much done too soon.

"I came on hard, real hard," he admitted. "My way of doing things is to go right after it. I never doubted for a minute, as soon as I could get baseball people like Charlie Fox and Gordon Goldsberry around me, that the Cubs were gonna be all right."

But matters weren't hunky-dory between Green and Cub fans. Like Sinatra, the general manager did things his way. Intent on "Building a New Tradition," he fired some longtime Cub employees, insisted the park needed lights, and shook up a

Dallas Green—the "New Tradition" is in place.

The Wrigley Field bleacher entrance gets spruced up in the early days of Dallas Green's regime. New paint is visible on the left.

storm that produced slow results and instant opposition.

"Everybody forgot the first word of our slogan was 'Building,'" he said. "All I heard in Chicago was 'Huh, the New Tradition is a 71–91 [1983] record for the Cubs. Dallas Green doesn't know anything.' It hurt that I didn't have the same kind of respect as a baseball man here that I had in Philadelphia. I'm aware it looked like we hadn't accomplished a helluva lot in two years, except I knew in my heart we had. The farm system and scouting were revitalized and we had a better 25-man roster than this town has seen in a long time.

"I wanted to make people understand the Cubs don't accept losing anymore," Green pointed out. "My trouble was I have a big mouth and I pop off about a lot of things. The Cubs were awful in my first year, and a lot of negative things had to be said. If my baseball people feel something has to be done, I'm the guy who has to do it, so I stand up and take the heat.

"The people in Chicago, fans and media, were resistant to any kind of change. They didn't want me to trade anybody, because they were Cub players. I was glad to get rid of some guys, but I felt I couldn't make a mistake in that first year. They all knew better than me what the Cubs needed, but nobody made an effort to find out what I was really like, or how I work."

Because he knew the players and the organization, most of Green's early dealings were with the Phillies. That drew still more backlash, labeling his team "the Midwest Philly Cubs." Nobody—not even Green—suspected that his January 27, 1982, trade with the Phils would give Chicago the cornerstone of a contending Cub team for the next decade.

THE TRADE OF THE DECADE

The unknown gem on the diamond, of course, was Ryne Sandberg, the kid who was supposed to be a throw-in on the deal which sent Ivan DeJesus to the Phillies for Larry Bowa in a shortstop swap. Green wanted Sandberg, and hung in there until it happened, but did not regard the minor-league infielder as a potential superstar.

"I'm not that smart," Green said. "We looked at Ryne as maybe a center fielder, a kid who could run and generate some excitement. I knew Bowa and [Phils' owner] Bill Giles had popped off at each other in the paper, so they had to get rid of him. We had an edge, because the Phillies needed a quality shortstop like DeJesus.

"I just kept pounding the fact that we were the poor cousins," Green outlined the strategy that finally pulled off the big steal. "We talked about other young players in their system, and I almost settled for somebody else, but credit Gordy Goldsberry for telling me to go after Sandberg.

"With the Phillies' experienced infield, Ryne wasn't going to play for them. I told them sending the kid back to the minors would kill him, and kept hammering away until we got it done."

That kind of perseverance came in handy when Green set out to beg, borrow, or steal a reliable corps of starting pitchers, the Cubs' critical lack. One by one, he welded links in the chain; Steve Trout came from the White Sox and Dick Ruthven came from the Phils in 1983. Then Green rolled up his sleeves for some moves that virtually assured him that an award for 1984 Executive of the Year would accompany him home to the family farm in West Grove, Pennsylvania, 40 miles from Philadelphia.

SIZZLING SWAPS

For openers, Green pried Scott Sanderson loose from Montreal in an off-season deal, before astounding the baseball world by getting two more starters in 19 days. The arrival of those right-handers—Dennis Eckersley on May 25 and Rick Sutcliffe on June 13—meant that what had been a dream for Cub fans suddenly had become possible. Green, a dealer in facts instead of emotion, realized that the new five-man starting rotation meant the end of prolonged losing streaks.

"What the Eckersley trade did was stop us from

having to send the 'maybe' guy out as the fourth starter," he said. "Maybe we got a good game out of Rick Reuschel or Chuck Rainey, maybe not. Poor Lee Elia had to count on Fergie Jenkins as the ace of his staff. When our starters walk to the mound now, the Cubs think they can win."

Of course, some unpopular moves had to be made, like releasing Jenkins when he was only 16 wins shy of the magic 300 victory total. Then, in '84, he traded popular Bill Buckner after benching him in favor of Leon Durham.

The general manager had one goal in mind. "Maybe some people wouldn't have made those changes, but I felt all along this club had a chance to go places," Green explained. "I didn't have a five-year plan. If the opportunity to win it all is there, you have to grab it. The key thing is that we had some quality people like Buckner, Bill Campbell, Mel Hall, and Joe Carter to trade away for the pitchers we needed. When Ruthven and Sandberg came up hurt early in the season, that was the signal to get out there and do something."

Green did something, but what he didn't do almost derailed the Cub Express. In his moment of triumph, after stealing Sutcliffe, pitcher George Frazier, and catcher Ron Hassey from the Indians, Green forgot that Cub outfielders Hall and Carter hadn't cleared NL waivers. That meant that they couldn't go to Cleveland or anywhere else except limbo.

"I butchered that up pretty good," Green admitted. "I've been in the game long enough to know that you pay for your mistakes. Fortunately, Cleveland wanted to keep the deal in place and they worked with us to make sure, even if we couldn't get the waivers. We would have delivered Hall and Carter later and probably given the Indians a player or two to get through until then."

It was embarrassing, but with the help of Cleveland GM Phil Seghi's class act ("A deal is a deal"), the dust finally settled, despite bitter blasts at Green from Hall and Carter. Their acrid comments got big play in the papers and on radio and TV, making it obvious to Green that (a) his work in swinging the splendid trade had been overlooked and (b) many fans were waiting for the 1984 Cubs to collapse, just as they had in 1969. "Now that we're winning, some people in Chicago are still doubting Thomases," Green said. "The 1969 Cubs? They lost, like the 1964 Phillies."

Green was a relief pitcher for the 1964 Phils, as

General manager Dallas Green's grin shows what he thinks of slugger Leon Durham's announcement that he'll donate $750 to Chicago High Schools for each Wrigley Field homer he hits.

painful a memory in Philadelphia as the '69 Cub cave-in is for Chicago. With the NL pennant wrapped for delivery, the Phillies suddenly collapsed, blowing their fat lead.

"We weren't revered in Philadelphia, if you remember," Green recalled. "We didn't even want to admit we were part of the 1964 Phils. After their careers, those guys made a living on being 1969 Cubs. It's incredible."

AT LAST, A GOOD GUY

So is Dallas Green, an incredibly honest man. After this season's breakthrough, he can't help noticing how his popularity has soared in Chicago.

"If you win, the fans think you're a good guy," Green said with a resigned shrug. "When the Cubs were losing, I was a bad guy. I don't want anybody to kiss my ring. I just want to be perceived as a baseball man who's done a job for this organization."

Still, the scars are there, and they won't go away, because mental scars are the hardest to heal. "The thing that bothered me most was trying to change a recognizably horsebleep baseball situation in Chicago, and nobody gave us a shot—until the day the Cubs started winning," Green said. "They wanted to jam it down my throat. They didn't want to see that the Cubs were a better team."

So it shouldn't surprise anyone that Green's first world championship, with the 1980 Phillies, will always be Number 1 in in his heart. "I grew up in the Philadelphia scene," he said. "Nothing's going to touch that experience. Nothing."

Regardless of his innermost feelings, getting it done in Chicago is Green's main priority now. He faces the challenge of preventing the Cubs from being one-season wonders by deterring Sutcliffe, Trout, Eckersley, pleasant surprise Rich Bordi, and first baseman Leon Durham from going the free-agent route. A staggering amount of money will be involved, especially for Cy Young shoo-in Sutcliffe.

"They have to declare free agency first, but I'm sure we'll get the opportunity to sign most of them before then," Green declared. "The fact that we're not afraid to spend money and reward production has changed the feel of the Cubs in baseball."

Getting it done has been almost an obsession with Green since boyhood in Lyndalia, Delaware, his sights were set on a major-league career. However arm problems prevented the pitcher from bettering a 20–22 lifetime mark. The trivia question for Green's career stems from 1963, when he served up Jimmy Piersall's 100th career homer, then yelled "Bush!" and other four-letter words while Piersall celebrated by running the bases backwards.

Today the front-runners who once bayed for Green's scalp are petitioning him to stay in Chicago. The alarm bell rang when Philadelphia writers noted with interest that the Phillies had left the general manager's chair open in a front-office reshuffle. Just turned 50, Green confessed to thoughts of returning to the area where he, his wife Sylvia, and four children still have roots.

"I have a job to do here, with two years left on my contract," said Green. "I intend to honor it, but all the talk I've heard of a big job opening up hasn't materialized."

The man most likely to determine Green's future is the one who went out on a limb to bring him to Chicago. Andy McKenna, the Cubs' board chairman, stuck with Green through thin and thin, confident he could build a winner. In less than three years, his judgment paid off.

"We'd like to extend the contract," McKenna said. "There are no problems I'm aware of. We'll sit down after the season and talk it over."

THE PRICE OF VICTORY

When Green says that the Cubs are willing to spend some money to keep players happy, he means it. During his term as Cub GM, he's been the architect of some mind-boggling contracts. Most have paid off.

An ironic slice of Cub history in the making in Kansas City during the 1980 World Series: Phillies' manager Dallas Green (top left) and Royals' manager Jim Frey discuss ground rules with umpire Harry Wendlestedt.

Ferguson Jenkins was an expensive flop for the Cubs in 1983. Jenkins was working on a new two-year contract, calling for a base salary of $375,000 in both 1983 and 1984. He also got a $50,000 signing bonus, but that wasn't all. The right-hander had a bonus clause in the contract that paid him $500 extra for each inning pitched from 1 to 100, and $1,000 per inning from 101 to 200 frames worked.

Since Jenkins hurled 167⅓ innings in '83, he pocketed $117,000 extra in bonus money. Along with salary and signing bonus, the Cubs paid him a total of $542,000 for a 6–9 record and 4.30 ERA. In addition, Jenkins got half of his 1984 salary when the Cubs released him.

"Yes, baseball payrolls are staggering," said McKenna. "It's the way things are for every club, and anybody who's naive about that shouldn't be in the business.

"Fortunately, the Cubs aren't paying off a lot of expensive contracts for players no longer here. Dallas Green inherited a couple, for Ken Reitz and Mike Tyson, that we had to swallow when they were released, and Jenkins just for this year."

But the contracts of stars on all teams, including the Cubs, call for eye-popping salary and bonus amounts. Third baseman Ron Cey has the best deal on the Cubs. Cey's contract, signed in January 1983, covers five years. He got a $500,000 signing bonus, plus attendance and performance bonuses. Cey will earn $800,000 base salary for 1984; $850,000 for 1985; $900,000 for 1986; and $950,000 for 1987. Each year, $150,000 of the salary is deferred, with interest. Cey also earned a $100,000 bonus when 1984 Cub attendance moved past the 1.5 million mark. If he is named most valuable player for any playoff or World Series during the length of the contract, Cey will get an extra $100,000. Finally, he'll be paid $300,000 more if the Cubs trade him before next year, and lesser amounts if it happens later.

Catcher Jody Davis has come a long way since 1982, when his salary was $80,000, plus a $50,000 bonus. His three-year contract, running through 1985, calls for a base salary of $215,000. But Davis earned $110,000 in bonus money last season, and his 1985 base pay will increase by the amount of bonuses he earned in 1984.

That should be a healthy amount. Davis gets a $10,000 bonus for games caught, starting with 70 and going to 150, a maximum of $90,000 extra. He also has an attendance clause worth $45,000 more—$10,000 for an attendance 1.4 million, $15,000 for 1.5 million, and $20,000 for 1.6 million. Other MVP and performance clauses could boost the total.

Baseball contracts are leaning toward performance clauses, so Dennis Eckersley's is an exception. The last year of the contract he signed with Boston in 1979 calls for a $270,000 salary, with a $400,000 up-front bonus. Another $900,000 in deferred salary bonus completes the five-year pact.

When Sandberg and Davis made the NL All-Star team in 1984, it was worth something extra. Along with a $600,000 base salary in Sandberg's new contract, he will draw a $30,000 bonus for appearing in 145 games, $35,000 for 600 plate appearances, and $20,000 for being selected an All-Star.

On the other end of the scale, Thad Bosley, who made a modest $70,000 in 1982, worked on a split contract last season that paid him $40,000 if he stayed in the majors, but just $3,300 a month for time in the minors. Rich Bordi, an unsung Cub hero, figures to get a new contract worth considerably more than the $35,000 and small bonus he earned in 1983.

But these are exceptions to the 1983 major league average salary of $572,105 for first basemen and $457,789 for outfielders. Dallas Green agrees the trend is in one direction—straight up. "It's not going to quit," he said. "To compete for players, you have to pay the price."

OTHER CUB SALARIES

Pitchers			
YEAR	PLAYER	BASE PAY	BONUS
1983	Warren Brusstar	$130,000	$75,000
1984	Dennis Eckersley	$270,000	
1983	George Frazier	$100,000	$25,000
1984	Dick Ruthven	$650,000	
1984	Scott Sanderson	$500,000	
1983	Lee Smith	$260,000	$90,000
1983	Tim Stoddard	$300,000	$29,000
1984	Rick Sutcliffe	$900,000	
1983	Steve Trout	$250,000	$15,000
Infielders			
YEAR	PLAYER	BASE PAY	BONUS
1983	Leon Durham	$350,000	
1983	Ron Hassey	$310,000	
1983	Richie Hebner	$265,000	
1984	Tom Veryzer	$210,000	$125,000
Outfielders			
YEAR	PLAYER	BASE PAY	BONUS
1983	Bob Dernier	$115,000	$27,500
1983	Jay Johnstone	$200,000	$10,000
1984	Gary Matthews	$600,000	
1983	Keith Moreland	$290,000	$70,000
1983	Gary Woods	$110,000	$30,000

4
OVER THE RAINBOW WITH RICK, RUFE, SCOTTY, AND ECK

SUTCLIFFE: KING OF THE HILL

Rick Sutcliffe is Chicago's Jolly Red-Bearded Giant.

No wonder he's happy. In the space of a few months, the towering right-hander hit the jackpot by escaping from the Cleveland Indians and assuring himself a new contract worth about $7.5 million. That's a much bigger win than even the Cubs' Daily Double, Bob Dernier and Ryne Sandberg, rang up all season in Wrigley Field. Sutcliffe wasted no time joining them in the winners' circle after the Indians traded him to Chicago on June 15, along with reliever George Frazier and catcher Ron Hassey.

The benign Sutcliffe appearance can be, and often is, misleading. Scratch the surface slightly and you'll find one of the last angry men, at least when it comes to pitching. Try to stop 6'7", 220-pound Rick Sutcliffe from doing what he does best and you'll have a fight on your hands. Anyone brave—or foolhardy—enough to challenge him had best bring along the Bears' defensive line. Off the field, Sutcliffe is a genial, friendly bear of a man. But when it comes to baseball, he is a tough, imposing perfectionist. Want proof? Just ask Dodger manager Tom Lasorda. Told he had no role in the Dodgers' 1981 playoff rotation, Sutcliffe trashed Lasorda's office. The pitcher refuses to wear his Los Angeles World Series ring and accepted being traded to Cleveland soon after the season ended.

Rick Sutcliffe: Move over, Cy Young.

A painful bout with root canal surgery, the trauma of watching the last-place Indians stagger under pop flies, and the prospect of pitching in a pennant race instead of comatose Cleveland Stadium made Sutcliffe react as though the trade to the Cubs had been a parole. He couldn't resist a

Sutcliffe draws a bead on a batter and the 1984 NL Cy Young Award.

Young Rick Sutcliffe can't keep his mind off baseball, even during the 1981 strike.

NO MORE LOSERS

Life and baseball are full of contradictions, and the happy Cub-Sutcliffe marriage ranks as one of them. Last winter, while exploring his chances of going anywhere—well, almost anywhere—to get away from Cleveland, Sutcliffe spurned the Cubs, refusing even to consider joining them. "The Cubs were not a contender last winter, but they are now," said Sutcliffe's agent, Barry Axelrod, explaining the pitcher's change of heart. "Rick is glad to be there and he wants to stay."

"I won't be fulfilled as a pitcher until I play a part in winning a World Series," Sutcliffe said as soon as the Cubs pried him loose from the Indians. "That's why I'm so glad to be here. I'm through playing for losers."

The new ace of the Cub staff wasn't exactly a poverty case when he arrived toting a one-year $900,000 contract. But Sutcliffe promptly proved he was a bargain, becoming the stopper the Cubs needed. He reeled off a string of victories, turning Cub Fever into an epidemic and demonstrating that he's one of baseball's best flingers.

In today's insane baseball numbers game, a hard-throwing 28-year-old pitcher who wins seven of every 10 decisions is worth plenty. Sutcliffe hoisted himself into the top tax bracket with talent, and Cub fans stormed the box office to see him.

TOTAL COMMAND

In his first start on June 20 against the Pirates, Sutcliffe breezed into the ninth inning with a 4–0 lead. But then the Cardiac Cubs yielded three runs. Lee Smith had to repel a Pirate raid, saving the 4–3 victory by retiring dangerous Bill Madlock with the bases loaded.

More often than not, Sutcliffe is in total command. In his Wrigley Field debut five days later, he blanked the Cards 5–0, fanning 14. Such gems established him as kingpin of the Cub staff, with injuries and other problems affecting other starters: Scott Sanderson and Dick Ruthven had serious ailments to overcome while Dennis Eckersley and Steve Trout grappled with bouts of inconsistency. Through it all, Sutcliffe was the anchor, keeping the Cubs atop the NL East by preventing extended losing streaks.

After the strapping right-hander lasted only five innings against the Reds on August 18 to get cred-

twinge of sympathy for Mel Hall and Joe Carter, sentenced to replace him. "If this team were the Titanic, I wonder how many players would let women and children into the lifeboat first," Sutcliffe summed up many of his ex-teammates' eagerness to flee the ragtag Indians.

Not that he needed more incentive to win for the Cubs, but a parting blast from the bitter Hall added some: "Who is Rick Sutcliffe?" Hall demanded. "Our team was like a family, and now they've disrupted it."

Cub fans soon discovered the answer to Hall's petulant query. Sutcliffe's brilliant pitching gradually calmed their fears of a 1969-style foldup.

He's not playing peek-a-boo, just hide-and-seek with batters in a 7-2 win over the Reds, Sutcliffe's 11th straight since joining the Cubs.

"This club knows I won't always have great stuff like a Sandy Koufax or a Nolan Ryan, but they also know they're going to get everything I have whenever I pitch," he added. "My biggest problem in Cleveland was not pitching, because the Indians won 70 percent of the games I started. The rest of the time, it was hard for me to watch."

His outlook, like his 4–5 pretrade record, has flip-flopped. "Now you could put pompons in my hand and call me a cheerleader when I'm in the dugout," Sutcliffe admitted. "Winning is the best part, but the fans have turned Wrigley Field into a circus and it's fun just being in the park. These Chicago fans are amazing."

Can he break his concentration to savor crowd reaction during a game? "Players really can't get involved in that until it's all over," he replied. "And yet it's a great feeling to know all that enthusiasm is for us. If the Cubs are five runs down and the leadoff man gets on base, 40,000 people are up, giving us a standing ovation, trying to get something going.

"For me, it was enough just leaving a team 25 games behind to pitch for one in first place," Sutcliffe pointed out. "My World Series ring from

Giving it his best shot on the bases, Sutcliffe barrels into San Diego's catcher Terry Kennedy. He was out at the plate.

it for a 13–11 Cub victory, he complained of getting too much rest. His demand for four days between starts, rather than five, was cut off at the pass by manager Jim Frey.

"Rick was getting pressure from people he shouldn't have been listening to," Frey explained. "He's too good a guy to let outside influences get in the way. Besides, I don't want five starters telling me when they should pitch."

The "outside influences" included a hint from his agent that a Cy Young Award would make him even more marketable, but after meeting with Frey, Sutcliffe agreed to stick to pitching and leave the masterminding to his manager. "I get paid to pitch and Jim Frey gets paid to manage," he said.

It was an ideal arrangement, because the big man knew exactly what he was doing on the mound. "In Cleveland, I had to try and shut the other guys out until the Indians scored," Sutcliffe explained his approach to pitching. "I have the same goal with the Cubs: just hang up that zero in the top of the first and give our hitters a chance to go to work.

the [1981] Dodgers doesn't mean anything, because I wasn't in on the games. Right here with the Cubs this year may be the only chance I'll ever get.

"This team was in first place when I got here and they have unbelievable comeback ability," he noted. "The Cubs have the hitting and pitching to go all the way, but we have to keep pushing each other down the stretch. The guys who don't do it will have to sit and watch."

Obviously, not being in the thick of things is Sutcliffe's biggest fear. "Everybody thinks they're going to win in the spring, but at the end, only one team is still there," Sutcliffe said. "I want the Cubs to be that team."

SCOTTY COMES HOME

Scott Sanderson feels just as strongly about winning. He came home this year to pitch for the Cubs, returning to his boyhood bailiwick, north suburban Northbrook. It was both a happy and painful homecoming.

Sanderson: At home.

Scott Sanderson proves the Cubs got a good deal in landing him from Montreal. The home-grown product shackled the Cards 6-1 on April 18, yielding only six hits.

Sanderson became a key starter, getting out of the gate quickly after the Cubs landed him from the Montreal Expos last December 7 by spinning consecutive two-hit wins, but trouble soon loomed. At 27, the slender right-hander was suddenly confronted with the jarring possibility that his career might be over.

What was diagnosed as back muscle spasms, a day-to-day ailment, stubbornly refused to go away. Sanderson pitched to two batters on May 15 in Cincinnati, then had to leave the game. He wound up in traction, enduring a series of painful recurrences along with x-rays showing no evidence of spinal disc injury.

Those assurances didn't ease the pain or remove doubts that it might be something chronic, but Sanderson pushed himself in a reconditioning program supervised by Cub trainer Tony Garafolo. Speeding up the timetable by ignoring advice not to run, he came off the disabled list to beat the

Giants July 6 with a strong effort in San Francisco's chilly fog. The troublesome back spasms continued to flare up, but Sanderson refused to take it easy.

"If the Lord says it's over, then it's over, so I haven't tried to ease back into pitching," he said. "If I get hurt again, I get hurt. All I can do is work to strengthen those back muscles."

Catcher Jody Davis knew, better than most people, how much pain Sanderson underwent while trying to get back in the groove despite severe discomfort on the mound. "After Scotty puts something extra on a pitch, I can see him flinch," Davis said.

"A lot of guys on this team are not 100 percent healthy, so it's not a big deal," Sanderson responded. "My back bothers me, but I can still pitch."

Despite the unexpected back misery, the three-way deal that brought Sanderson to the Cubs has been a plus for the team. His work in a starting role eased the sting of giving up Carmelo Martinez, a promising young slugger.

TOUGH ENOUGH

Sanderson's fortitude never has been questioned in six National League seasons after a fast rise through the Expos' farm system. "I knew Scotty was a competitor when he was just a kid, pitching in the Venezuelan winter league in 1977," said Cubs pitching coach Billy Connors, recalling a hitter who, angered by Sanderson's high, hard one that backed him off the plate, stalked menacingly toward the mound, waving his bat. "Sanderson drilled him in the back with his next pitch," Connors said. "Then the fight started."

To their delight, Cub teammates found that Sanderson wouldn't hesitate to protect them when an enemy pitcher knocked somebody down. After the Mets' Ed Lynch plunked Keith Moreland, triggering the August 7 Wrigley Field brawl, Sanderson retaliated immediately on the Mets' Kelvin Chapman. The umpires had warned both teams and managers to cease the dusters, but Sanderson did what he had to do and promptly got the heave-ho, along with Frey. Since Sanderson hadn't lasted five innings, reliever Tim Stoddard got credit for the victory. That didn't bother Sanderson. "Anybody taking shots at our guys will pay the price," he said.

"He fools you," Frey said with a grin. "Scotty's so clean-cut, nobody expects him to be tough enough out there. He is."

THE HARD WORK PAYS OFF

The Sanderson family moved to the Chicago area when Scott was 12, and the big kid went on to pitch Glenbrook North High School to the 1974 Illinois state baseball championship. Passing up a Kansas City Royals draft bid, he went to Vanderbilt University and made the U.S. baseball team in the Pan-American games of 1976. The young fireballer earned his spot by yielding one run in 35 innings, a tip-off of the ability that moved him up to the majors less than two seasons after signing with the Expos.

But Sanderson's six years on the Montreal staff were plagued by injuries and the power-packed Expos' failure to dominate the NL East despite an abundance of talent. Ironically, the worst injury happened in Wrigley Field on July 4, 1983, when Sanderson tore ligaments and severed a right thumb muscle in a fall. Typically, he refused to write off the season, coming back to win two of three starts in September. Such true grit was rewarded with a ticket to Chicago. He and wife Cathleen were happy to return.

"So the effort paid off," Sanderson noted. "Even if it hadn't, that's the only way I can do things."

RAINBOW FINDS HIS POT OF GOLD

The Cub starter with most to prove this season was Steve Trout, the erratic left-hander who kept slipping out of the groove in 1983 during his first spin on the North Side turntable. Trout became the pet reclamation project of pitching coach Connors, and Connors's skillful touch reaped a bumper crop of results. Under his patient tutelage, Trout became a winning pitcher.

The big winner in Trout's belated induction to the ranks of consistent performers was Trout himself. The former problem child of the White Sox resembled a yo-yo, with a 10–14 record and 4.65 ERA in his Cub debut. General manager Dallas Green made it clear that that wouldn't do. "We need more from you," Green told Trout in spring training. "You're not a kid anymore and you can't live on potential."

The new Steve Trout, a winner.

Trout had more than erratic pitching to overcome. His reputation for being a flaky, overaged flower child, circa 1968, was enhanced by flowing locks, worn denims, and a shambling gait. An emotional type, Trout made things worse for himself by ignoring the media.

That was a carry-over from five frustrating years on the South Side, where Trout never lived up to the promise he displayed as a rookie. Mutual hostility reigned among White Sox manager Tony LaRussa, his coaches, and Trout. A trade was the only answer, and Green's failure to protect pitcher Ferguson Jenkins on the 1983 Cub roster opened the door. It produced a deal that sent Trout and Warren Brusstar to the Cubs for Randy Martz, Dick Tidrow, Scott Fletcher, and Pat Tabler. The smart money proclaimed it penance for Green and pennant for the Sox, but things look very different now.

UPHILL STRUGGLE

From boyhood, Trout had a tough act to follow, because his dad was Paul "Dizzy" Trout of the Detroit Tigers, an outstanding pitcher and a renowned storyteller. Dizzy had tamed the Cubs

After a full afternoon of close harmony, pitcher Steve Trout and catcher Jody Davis celebrate another nail in the Mets' coffin.

4–1 to win the fourth game of the 1945 World Series in Wrigley Field, 38 years before his son would pitch in the same park. Even before Steve graduated from Thornwood High School in South Holland, Illinois, the inevitable "Rainbow" nickname had been draped on him.

Small wonder that Trout faced a long, uphill struggle. Critics and cynics wrote him off when he couldn't win for the White Sox. Then the whispers began, speculating on the cause of his failures.

"Drugs," Trout said. "That was the convenient excuse. It annoys me, but I'm clean. I hurt my arm and couldn't pitch, so they thought I was laying down. I couldn't get past the fifth inning and they thought it was because of drugs.

"Everything except the real reason," Trout shrugged. "They never taught me how to pitch over there."

YEAR OF DECISION

When Trout came to spring training in 1984, a year of decision for his career, he found new Cub manager Jim Frey solidly in his corner. That vote of confidence was crucial in transforming the 27-year-old southpaw from an erratic thrower into a winning pitcher. "You can't associate all the stuff that went on with the other club in Chicago and what's happened now," Frey said. "Sometimes you have to let players mature and grow up."

After a year of groping with the Cubs, things finally began to happen for Trout. With Connors and Jody Davis honing his concentration, the left-hander began to repay the team's belief in him. He beat Mets' rookie phenom Dwight Gooden in the Cubs' home opener, no-hit the Braves for 7⅔ innings, weathered a midseason slump, and came through brilliantly in one of the most important games of the season.

In the opener of a Shea Stadium double-header July 29, Trout whitewashed the Mets 3–0 on just seven singles. His pet pitch, the sinker, had the frustrated home team beating the ball into the dirt for 17 ground outs, setting them up for a Cub sweep that turned the NL East race around. It was Trout's first shutout in almost four years, and his timing was perfect. Sanderson stopped New York 5–1 in the nightcap, pulling the Cubs within 1½ games of the division leaders.

Complete games are more important than shut-

outs," said Trout, reflecting his new-found maturity. "I'm just letting my pitching take over."

AN ECK OF A GOOD TIME

While Trout was finding the answer, Dennis Eckersley was still groping in his first National League season. He had stepped into a pressure cooker on May 25, when the Boston Red Sox traded him for longtime Cub favorite Bill Buckner.

The stocky right-hander had tried to come back too soon from a sore shoulder in 1983 and had been stung by criticism. The result was a 9–13 record and 5.61 ERA, leading Boston fans to believe that he was washed up before the Red Sox unloaded him to the Cubs.

Eckersley reacted emotionally in a farewell session with Boston writers. In recent seasons, critics had rapped Eckersley for his tendency to fade in late innings. He insisted he had been expected to produce miracles as the ace of a thin pitching staff.

"I want to get over to the other league and prove

Dennis Eckersley: The Hard Luck Kid.

I can still pitch," he said. "Last time I got traded [from Cleveland to the Red Sox in 1978], I really got juiced up."

Until Sutcliffe—another AL exile—came over to join him three weeks later, Eckersley found himself in a tough situation with the Cubs. He was expected to produce shutouts, the same burden that had caused him to press and overthrow the ball in Boston. Actually, the 6'2", 200-pound veteran performed well, but the Cubs did not seem to score runs with their usual efficiency when he was on the mound.

"Fans expect so much of you," Eckersley said. "It gets tiresome. I'm glad to be with the Cubs, but the same pressure is here. It's what we get paid for."

After years of frustration with the Indians and Red Sox, Eckersley insisted that the pressure didn't

Eckersley and Davis talk it over during a rough spot in a nationally televised 4-1 win over Atlanta.

bother him. "Who's counting?" Eckersley said, shrugging off a victory total lower than he deserved with the Cubs. "I haven't pitched on a winning team for six years, and this is terrific. Last season was so bad, I was ready to give up."

The move to Chicago was a good one for Eckersley, both personally and professionally. Turning 30 on October 3, he is young enough to tap the free-agent pot of gold awaiting veterans who are lucky enough to be paid for such riches.

Having survived his rocky period of adjustment, Eckersley became a stable cog in the five-man rotation. He liked it a lot more than the 1978 Red Sox array of Luis Tiant, Mike Torrez, Spaceman Bill Lee, and himself. "This Cub staff is better than that one was," Eckersley said. "Much better."

RUFUS RECOVERS

The senior Cub starter is 33-year-old Dick Ruthven, another product of Dallas Green's Philadelphia connection. And of all the comebacks on a winning team stitched together from others' discards, Ruthven's is the most amazing.

Even Green, a Ruthven admirer for years, was stunned by the veteran's quick recovery from major surgery to cure a shoulder ailment that could have ended his career. "Technically, he shouldn't be pitching at all," Green said. "I tell him, 'Rufus, you gotta be elated.' When they did the operation [May 23], the doctors told me the first of September was the earliest he could start to throw again. "I washed him off, but he worked his way back."

Ruthven's teammates were equally astonished. A 4–0 Cub defeat was normally no cause for clubhouse celebration in this upbeat season, but after the gritty right-hander lost to the San Diego Padres by that score on July 16, there was elation instead of depression. "I won't jump up and down when the Cubs lose, but there was a lot to be happy about in the way I pitched," Ruthven said.

Just unleashing the ball with big-league velocity only 54 days after the operation was a minor miracle. The problem, a shoulder muscle that had been pressing on an artery, blocking the blood flow to Ruthven's right arm, obviously had been cleared up.

"Before that, Rufus would run out of gas around the fourth inning," said catcher Jody Davis. "Today, he was still popping the ball in the eighth inning."

Dick Ruthven: The Comeback Kid.

That was all Ruthven needed to know. The strong, silent pitcher known to the Cubs as the Mountain Man had been prepared for the worst. "It was killing me," he confessed. "I wanted to give the Cubs their money back, because I knew how much I meant to the team.

"I never knew when the thing started," Ruthven said. "There was no pain or stiffness, but my arm would die after the fourth inning. My trademark used to be getting stronger as the game went on, and I'm excited about being able to pitch that way again."

Ruthven has enough inner strength to cope with the situation, even if it had meant the end of his career. He bounced back from being discarded by Phillies manager Pat Corrales and then being shipped to the Cubs on May 22, 1983, in a trade for left-handed reliever Willie Hernandez. "I tried not to let it get me down, but it did," Ruthven admitted. "I guess that just shows I'm human. It broke my spirit a little."

Becoming a Cub healed that wound and Ruthven's strong will did the same thing to his surgery scar, well ahead of schedule. The Mountain Man can still stand tall on the hill.

Catcher Jody Davis tells Ruthven that his complete-game victory was a gem.

5
CUBS FLY HIGH WITH FREY

Manager of the Year? Right off the bat in spring training, it didn't look like Jim Frey would last long enough with the 1984 Cubs to be named manager of the morning. What a false alarm that turned out to be. As soon as his red-hot team began to Frey the rest of the National League, it set victory-starved Chicago ablaze. Unlike the Great Chicago Fire of 1871, this conflagration was cause for celebration.

Celebration? It was more like resurrection. Without warning, a 38-year plague of glue-footed, candy-armed, dead-end baseball was lifted on the North Side, replaced almost overnight by a diamond, dugout, and bullpen full of eager over-achievers.

"The one thing I wanted to create on this team more than anything else was the idea of bringing 25 guys together, feeling they couldn't wait to get to the park," Frey explained. "We kept the ones who wanted to play and take pride in being Chicago Cubs.

"When I made a plan for improvement at home in Baltimore last winter, [that idea] was first on my list. I knew if we could get that across, winning would follow right behind."

Jim Frey ponders his next move in Shea Stadium. It must have been a good one, because the Cubs bombed the Mets 11-4.

31

"Now hear this, Cubs. Peerless leader Frey's talking. Go get 'em!"

An eager Frey gets his first look at Wrigley Field after being named Cubs' manager.

It took a smorgasbord of some old, some new, some begged, borrowed, or stolen players to don Cubs' blue, but when general manager Dallas Green got them, Frey knew what to do with them. He turned a dismal 7–20 Cactus League season into an asset by convincing his players that the team was better than anyone suspected. Before the Cubs left spring training, Frey had them believing March would be their only losing month of the season. He stopped the clubhouse bickering that escalated into a widely publicized fistfight between pitcher Dick Ruthven and outfielder Mel Hall with four words: "That's not professional conduct."

The Cubs soon discovered their manager was right on that score, so they concentrated on making final scores come out right. When things began to happen, it felt so good that they began to believe in both themselves and their skipper.

Not only could Frey's recycled miracle workers hit the ball prodigious distances, but they also could pitch and catch it with brisk efficiency. Best of all, these Cubs were no 30-day wonders like Bob Speake or Bill Faul, igniting brief sparks before fading into obscurity. When the 1984 Cubs made mistakes, they didn't brood or point accusing fingers at teammates. When they lost, they bounced back, higher and harder. In short, they were what Chicago fans had been pining for since 1945.

POSITIVE THINKING

What has all this to do with a slightly chubby, bespectacled 53-year-old named James Gottfried Frey? Everything.

He took the nuts and bolts of the erector set

dumped in his lap by Dallas Green, shook it well, added a heaping tablespoon of positive thinking, and Presto! A Cub winner, at last. In baseball, the rare man capable of doing that can write his own ticket to manage anywhere.

Jim Frey calls himself a professional. He got the job done in Chicago by applying the experience, horse sense, and seat-of-the-pants baseball knowledge earned in 33 years of on-the-bench training. From Paducah, Kentucky, in the minors to the Orioles of Baltimore mastermind Earl Weaver, the Kansas City Royals, and the New York Mets in the majors, Frey's been around. There were too many whistle stops to count in between, but he worked, listened, and learned in all of them. That's how he knew a first priority in Chicago had to be demolishing the myth that summer heat and day baseball in Wrigley Field could prevent the Cubs from becoming contenders.

"When I played in the Texas League, it was over 100 degrees almost every day," Frey said. "One year, I played every inning of every game, then went to winter ball and played every inning. So I don't want to hear that bunk about players getting too tired from playing in the sun. It's just a built-in excuse for losing. Major leaguers can play under any conditions."

Those who play for Frey certainly do. The Cubs quickly closed the talent gap between themselves and the rest of the National League, but even before the players realized what they could do, the new manager felt confident. "I think our club was a little bit abused by the media in spring training," Frey said. "Especially the defense, one of our main strengths this year. It was obvious the hitters were there and after the first half, of course, the pitching became a lot stronger.

"But one of the things that's been overlooked

Frey tries to make umpire John Kibler see the light in Philadelphia, insisting that Bob Dernier should be allowed to score on Gary Matthews's ground-rule double. Guess who won the debate.

right from the start was the consistent, if not spectacular, defense played by the Cubs. We have not made a lot of costly errors. Up the middle, we've been outstanding.

"Sandberg is all by himself at second base, Jody Davis became a much better defensive catcher this year and Bob Dernier covers ground in center field to make the tough plays. Fans don't take into account that a team can't play consistent baseball without that kind of defense."

Frey has acquired the knack for deflecting the spotlight so that it shines on the players. His deft sense of humor soon convinced the media that the straightlaced appearance, enhanced by tinted glasses and hair combed straight back, was misleading. He's no somber man; when Frey talks baseball, it's both entertaining and enlightening.

Despite the scholarly look, the new field boss showed the Cubs he could—and would—back them up with deeds, as well as words. He didn't bother picking on anybody his own size on May 17 in Cincinnati, when the Reds' Dave Parker, 6'5" and 230-pounds, butted in while Frey was jawing at umpire Bob Engle. The 5'7" Frey told the hulking Parker to stuff it, and both men had to be restrained from swapping punches. The Cubs chuckled about the mismatch, but from then on, the skipper had their respect.

Still, Frey disdains magical solutions or so-called shortcuts to getting results. He's convinced the only right way is to put good players on the field and keep them hungry. "Winning is the thing that solves all problems," Frey said. "At the tail end of winning, everybody wants to come up with all kinds of theories and psychology that didn't have a darn thing to do with it. The thing I preached all spring was playing hard, not with crazy emotion, but under control. Nobody can measure the kind of energy you get from that, and how important it is."

The Cubs responded with a daring, aggressive, come-from-behind style that captivated fans and intimidated foes. Ordered by their manager not to be "safety-first guys," they soon discovered how to put pressure on the opposing defense with intelligent gambles that worked. And whenever the Cubs pulled out another close game with those tactics, Frey scoffed at the notion that some kind of witchcraft was involved.

"Anybody who wants to manage a major-league team has to have enough experience and confidence in his own ability," he said. I'm not one to get all shook up when things go a little sour. That's the time for the manager and his coaches to show some real stability. While we were in the middle of that big [11-game] losing streak in spring training, I called a meeting and told them that when I put the right guys on the field, the Cubs were a good ballclub, a very good one," he recalled. "I could see that from the beginning, so I didn't worry about exhibition games, although I never expected to lose that many in a row.

"I had to try a lot of players I'd never seen before," the rookie NL pilot pointed out. "As soon as we got Dernier and Matthews in that [March 27] trade, I knew our defense would be solid.

"So was the hitting, but there was still some question mark about the starting pitchers at that point," Frey said. "Early in the year, we were winning with our bats and a lot of guys coming off the bench to help us struggle through a bunch of high-run games. After Dallas [Green] swung those trades to get Dennis Eckersley and Rick Sutcliffe, we won our share without the big hitting. Then we bounced back with the bats. You never know how the Cubs will get the job done, but as long as we do it, who cares?"

DON'T AX HIM WHY

That was precisely the go-get-'em attitude Green wanted in a manager. Predecessor Lee Elia's emotional approach had not welded the Cubs into a close-knit unit or produced many victories. "I was looking for someone like Jim," Green said. "A low-key baseball man who came up through a farm system, handles the press well, and doesn't back away from controversy."

That was a blueprint of Frey, who got fired as the Kansas City Royals' manager because he refused to be bulldozed by his players. Astonishingly, that happened less than one full season after he had led the Royals to their first World Series, a 1980 matchup with Philadelphia, then managed by Green. The Phillies won, but Green admired the way his rival handled the American League champs.

Neither man suspected that fate would reunite them in Chicago a few years later, to become architects of the Cub turnabout. Frey was demoralized when the ax fell on him in Kansas City on

A big moment in Jim Frey's career: The ex-coach of the Orioles steps up to his first managing post, taking over the Kansas City Royals on October 24, 1979. He's flanked by Kansas City brass John Schuerholt at left and Joe Burke.

August 31, 1981, just three weeks after he had managed the AL All-Stars. Instead of being bitter, he looks back on it as a learning experience for the Cub challenge.

"I had differences with Royals' management over trades, but the Willie Wilson incident was the biggest thing," Frey reflected. "I reminded him about our sport-coat rule for traveling, so he got mad and went home. All of a sudden, there was dissension among the players."

Ludicrous as it seems, the missing coat ended up costing Frey his job. It also taught him a valuable lesson. "I found out there's a human element to managing," Frey summed up his self-analysis. "I can't be a buddy to the players, but I try to spend more time with them and be aware of their personal problems.

Sometimes I overlook those things," he admitted. "I'm not the kind of guy who's a worrier. When you lose, go home and get a good night's sleep, come back the next day and start over. If a club does that, they can shake off tough losses."

Frey drove home that message when Cubs floundered in training camp and again when their early-season bubble was burst by the Phillies in a humiliating four-game series sweep in Wrigley Field. That knocked the cocky Cubbies out of first place, and those who had seen it happen all too many times figured the mid-June swoon was on. Instead, Frey used it to make his team stronger and more resilient, the same way he had turned the Kansas City crisis into a step forward.

"They might have been thinking everything would go our way without extra effort," he shrugged. "Getting swept should show us there are no gifts in this league. Now we'll start to get motivated."

Other Cub managers had been saying the same thing for what seemed like centuries, but this time, the players really listened. Better yet, they turned Frey into a prophet and the Cubs into a profit-making organization for the first time in years. When the dam of pent-up emotion was swept away by the flood of adulation from true believers and new believers in every state of the union, even the taciturn Frey was jolted by its intensity.

"Seeing those fans lined up for tickets early in the morning, and getting letters from all over the country," he said with a rueful shake of the head. "It's really something. I've been trying to keep things low-key in the clubhouse. But just before we went on that important Eastern trip [July 23–29 to face the Phillies and the Mets], I had a little meeting and told them we can't deny anymore that we're in a pennant race. The one thing I didn't want was for all of the attention and all of the hype to change our style. I asked the players to avoid doing things differently. All we needed was the same enthusiasm and aggressiveness the Cubs showed me early in the year.

"This is no time to be getting conservative," Frey reminded his players. "Let's keep doing things our way. If you slack off now, other teams will knock you down."

The Phillies and Mets tried to do just that, but failed. In a triumphal tour of Philadelphia and New York, the sizzling Cubs won five of seven pressure-packed games, soon turning the NL East into a one-horse race.

Frey and his Cubs found a turned-on, tuned-in Chicago awaiting their return in a state of semi-hysteria. A man who had to struggle for everything he got in baseball, Frey easily understood the reaction.

"After all that time in the minors, I finally got a coaching job with the Orioles in 1970, and they won the World Series," he said. "I felt a sense of gratitude, and it helps me realize how much these fans want the same thing to happen here.

"I was lucky to get another shot at managing, especially in Chicago, where the owners are committed to winning," Frey added, shuffling through the index cards he uses to keep track of how his hitters fare against opposing pitchers. "Once we got going, I knew Wrigley Field would be packed every day. I don't believe any other team in the majors has a following like the Cubs do. Everywhere we go, they're in the stands, rooting for us."

FIRST CLASS COACHES

Frey had some capable help in giving Cub fans what they wanted. He inherited excellent coaches, including Billy Connors, who had handled the

A younger Don Zimmer, chaw in place, prepares to take his practice cuts 24 years ago in Wrigley Field.

Kansas City pitching staff for Frey in the pennant-winning year. A new third-base traffic cop, Don Zimmer, and a new bullpen coach, Johnny Oates, joined holdovers Ruben Amaro and John Vukovich to complete the coaching lineup.

BILLY'S NO BULLY

Connors came to the Cubs in 1982 with a reputation for being a pitchers' pitching coach. The mileage he squeezed from a ragtag North side staff in that rebuilding stage proved his worth. A well-traveled minor leaguer who played for 12 different clubs in a decade, Connors hung up a lifetime 0–2 record in the majors after cups of coffee with the Cubs and Mets. Like Frey, he mastered his profession in tank towns, learning how to pass along the theory of pitching to others much better than he could practice it. Along with a genial personality, Connors' vast store of mound lore made him a natural.

"I live and die with my pitchers and they know that," Connors said. "Sometimes you let them get away with a few things to see how far they'll go, and other times you have to jump on them.

Don Zimmer, a scrappy competitor in his playing days, can't hide admiration for the Reds' Pete Rose.

Coach Ruben Amaro plays straight man for Mel Hall after the Cub outfielder slammed a three-run triple in 1983, his last full season on the North Side.

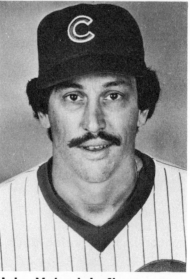

Billy Connors, arming the Cubs.

John Vukovich, first-rate first base coach.

John Oates, bullpen coach.

Pitchers will respond if they know you care."

They sure respond for Connors, at any rate. He relished the challenge of turning flamethrower Lee Smith into a relief standout and demolishing the "sink or drown" pitching myth that most baseball people believed about Wrigley Field.

"The old notion that you have to throw a sinker in Wrigley Field is a fallacy," Connors said. "For years, they taught it in the Cub organization, and Fred Martin [the pitching coach who tutored Bruce Sutter on his celebrated split-finger fast ball] had me work on it in the minors. Kids get it in their heads they have to throw sinkers and nibble around the plate in this park. If you're a nibbler in Wrigley Field, you get killed."

That was the advice Connors gave Smith, convincing him to come out of the bullpen belching smoke. "The first thing I told Lee was, 'If you want to make some money, hold the ball across the seams [the grip for a rising fastball] and let it fly.' " Connors related. "In the last few years, he's been a pretty good relief pitcher doing it that way."

Connors approaches each pitcher differently, and for most of them, he has a magic touch. For his pet project, Steve Trout, the right formula was laying it on the line.

"Rainbow, no more of your bull," Connors told the left-hander when they went to Florida last winter to iron out flaws in his delivery. "I'm fed up with working on you and getting nothing back."

Trout paid off the investment in full this season, becoming a consistent winner for the first time in his career. "I always figured the right guy would help me," Trout said. "That's Billy. He taught me to be patient and hang in there."

Connors has something to offer all pitchers besides baby-sitting for their egos. Throwing a baseball is an unnatural movement that causes severe stress. He breaks down the pitchers' deliveries on film and video tape, seeking ways to prevent sore arms. I'm a big believer in mechanics, because a smooth delivery takes strain off the arm," Connors said. "Basically, we want our pitchers to keep the ball down, throw strikes and make their pitches count. We finally got Trout in that groove by telling him to forget about the spitball he used to throw with the White Sox and stick to basic pitches."

When the other Cub pitchers saw the results Connors got, they lined up for tips. For instance, Connors helped Scott Sanderson to speed up his delivery, keeping the defense alert.

For Trout and the rest of the Cub staff, Connors provides the beginning, not the end, of the Rainbow.

Author Bob Logan and Jim Frey anticipate another "Cubs Win!" in Wrigley Field.

6
PASSING THE BUCK TO BULL, BOWA, AND PENGUIN

Baseball nicknames don't have to be accurate. Turkey Mike Donlin wasn't a turkey: he batted .333 lifetime. And Hollis "Sloppy" Thurston was actually a stylish dresser.

Leon "Bull" Durham is another example. The Cubs' first baseman does not resemble a bull, nor does he throw the bull. He's a friendly, soft-spoken gentleman, who knows his misleading label is just part of the game. Tradition dictates that any baseball player named Rhodes is a Dusty and any Durham is a Bull.

Maybe there were times Durham wanted to blow off steam with bull-like snorting, stomping, and pawing the turf, when it seemed things would never fall into place for him with the Cubs. If so, nobody knew. The strapping 27-year-old is not the type to sulk, pout, and dispense a load of bull when asked where he belongs on the field.

"I'm a natural first baseman," he'll tell you. It's my home, man. When they hit the ball to me, I can pick it. I can cover the ground. Becoming a first baseman again was the best thing that's happened to me in the majors. We knew the talent was here on the Cubs, and it was just a matter of putting it together in the right places. Jim Frey knows how to use his players."

Leon Durham: Noble Bull.

Beneath their own high-fives, happy Cubs Ryne Sandberg, Bull Durham, Ron Cey, and Jody Davis enjoy a 6-5 triumph over San Diego.

41

First base clearly was the right place for Durham, but there was a large, popular, mustachioed obstacle in his path, by the name of Bill Buckner. Besides being a first-rate first sacker in his own right, Billy Buck also had a seven-year grip on the affection of Wrigley Field fans for his hitting and hustling. He won the National League batting championship in 1980, assuring that newcomer Durham's only glimpse of first base for the next three years would be running there on a single.

BUCKNER BENCHED

The situation changed when repeated efforts to trade Buckner fell through in the winter and spring of 1984. Soon after the Cubs went to camp in Mesa, Arizona, Durham was awarded full-time status at first base and Buckner got the consolation prize—a seat on the bench. All the elements for a feud between the old order and the new were present, but it didn't happen, a credit to both players

The way things turned out in '84 made the decision seem clear-cut, although that's 20-20 hind-

Gary Matthews (top) escorts Durham into the dugout after Bull's homer rocketed the Cubs to another win.

The new and old order in Wrigley Field— Durham and Bill Buckner.

Bull bellows with glee after a two-run homer in Cincinnati, where he grew up. His proud mother, Mrs. Helen Cook, saw the blast.

sight. At the time it was controversial and questionable for a lifetime .300 hitter to cool his heels in training camp while the Cubs looked like a bad team. When their spring losing streak stretched to 11 in a row, howls of outrage could be heard all the way from Chicago.

It was another difficult time for Durham. The Bull came through it with the same cool, classy approach he had employed to survive Chicago crisis No. 1, the one that erupted when Durham was traded to the Cubs on December 9, 1980, along with Ken Reitz and Tye Waller, for relief kingpin Bruce Sutter.

A GIFT OF HOPE

The kid from Cincinnati had been taught very early how to cope by his mother, Mrs. Helen Cook, who raised a big family, six boys and four girls, by herself. Leon's outlook on life is ample evidence that she did a superb job. As soon as he became an established major leaguer, with a matching contract, Durham began donating money to Chicago high school athletic departments for each Wrigley Field homer he hit. The ante was $750 per round-tripper in 1984, and it replaced a lot of ragged

equipment for youngsters who hoped to follow in the Bull's footsteps.

"Just giving back something for all the good things that happened to me," said Durham, who was a three-letter standout at Cincinnati's Woodward High School before St. Louis drafted him in 1976. "It's the way my mother brought us up."

With that kind of class, Durham needed little time to melt fans' resentment in 1980 when Sutter was unloaded to the Cards because the Cubs couldn't afford the escalating salaries of such superstars. The rookie seemed to understand the wrath that would fall on him if he proved to be another bust. Even 20 years later, Cub fans still shuddered at the memory of the horrendous 1964 trade that sent Lou Brock to the Cards for Ernie Broglio.

I don't want to be the franchise," Durham pleaded his case. "Anybody they got for Sutter would face pressure, but it won't come from me.

While Dodger catcher Mike Scioscia labors in the rain, on-deck hitter Leon Durham keeps cool—and dry.

"I'll have to become an everyday player for the Cubs."

Durham made good on that promise immediately. His bat made a lot of noise, but he didn't, accepting his role in right field, and sometimes center, without complaining. Before long, the Bull's blend of character and talent made him one of the best-liked Cubs. Still, the team kept losing until this magical year, and Durham was one of the few blue chips they could flash in the trading market quest for pitching stability.

His career seemed ready for a rocket to superstardom in 1982, lifted into orbit by 22 homers, 90 RBI, and a .312 average, along with 28 stolen bases. That made Bull the first Cub to top 20 home

It's neither a bird nor a plane. It's SUPERBULL.

Durham and Gary Matthews welcome home Keith Moreland after his grand slam against the Expos. Glum catcher Gary Carter is shoved aside as palms slap and Wrigley Field rocks.

runs and steals in the same season since 1911, when Frank "Wildfire" Schulte hit 21 and stole 23. But a pulled hamstring, back spasms and a broken right thumb put his beef back in the corral the following year. Durham missed 64 games in 1983, falling off sharply in all departments. Had it not been for Durham's second straight NL All-Star berth, giving him a chance to play in the 50th anniversary Dream Game at Comiskey Park, the season would have been a complete wipeout.

Durham could have made a scapegoat out of since-deposed Cub manager Lee Elia, but that's not his style. Elia left himself open to criticism by ignoring the Bull's request to use a pinch runner and spare his sore hamstring.

"I told Lee to take me out, but I ended up running hard to score the winning run and I was out for three more weeks," he recalled. "I knew I was trying to come back too quick."

Typically, he leveled no criticism at the beleaguered Elia when it happened. The manager still was trying to live down an ill-advised, profane blast at Cub fans, unleashed before he had cooled off from a tough loss. The even-tempered Durham also didn't fault his wife, Angela, for suggesting contact lenses this spring, though he soon went back to the familiar spectacles.

"I couldn't pick up the rotation with contacts, to tell if the pitch was a breaking ball," Durham said. "Wearing glasses, I can see the stitches.

BULL'S BULLISH ON CUBS

Soon after, Durham could see his future looking brighter. Buckner was traded to Boston May 20 for pitcher Dennis Eckersley, and suddenly the Cubs found a bull market at first base and in first place.

"This is the best team I've ever played on," Durham said when the Cubs had recovered from briefly spinning their wheels, then shifted into high gear and roared off in pursuit of a first-ever divisional title. The injury bugaboo struck again June 23 in St. Louis, when Durham jammed his shoulder diving head-first into second base. Fortunately, it was not serious, and with Keith Moreland filling in at the initial sack, Durham didn't have to rush back prematurely this time.

When he returned, the Cubs came with a rush, blasting the Mets and Phillies out of their path. The Bull's major anxiety after that came during the week when his wife, overdue with the couple's first

baby, had to have labor induced in a Cincinnati hospital. He left the team briefly to be with her, and daughter Lauren Ashley Durham, a healthy nine pounds, was born August 31. Durham celebrated with a home run in Atlanta two days later.

"I was nervous about what my wife was going through, but we're really happy," Durham said. "How many people have a chance to get a new baby and a World Series ring in the same year?

THE PENGUIN: ONE TOUGH BIRD

Ron Cey already had one of each—a son, daughter, and a diamond-studded ring from the Dodgers' 1981 World Series victory. He also has a contract for about $1 million per year through 1987. Cey even has a stylish nickname, the Penguin, for his low center of gravity and short strides.

Now there's a man who has everything—including pain. Cey waded through a lot of mental distress when the Dodgers decided he was washed up, unloading him after a decade at third base. A

Ron Cey: Penguin Power.

Sometimes, the right pitch isn't there. Cey trudges back to the dugout after striking out.

few weeks before his 35th birthday, Cey was shipped to the Cubs on Jan. 20, 1983, for minor leaguers Vance Lovelace and Dan Cataline.

It was a slap in the face and a rabbit punch to the ego of a proud man. With 228 career homers, Cey was the all-time Los Angeles leader, ranking fourth behind Brooklyn Dodger sluggers Duke Snider (389), Gil Hodges (361), and Roy Campanella (242). Despite the fabulous deal extracted from the Cubs by agent Steve Schneider, Cey didn't make an easy transition from Hollywood to Ra-

venswood, on Chicago's North Side. He walked into a typically cold spring, getting off to an equally frigid start in 1983. Naturally, the new third baseman didn't get a red-hot reception from Wrigley Field customers aware of his overstuffed paycheck. Being separated from his family until the school year ended didn't make things any better.

"I didn't handle it the way I should have," Cey admitted of his sudden switch from celebrity in Los Angeles to futility in Chicago. "Everything was new all of a sudden—players, owners, fans."

But Cey knew only one way to deal with adversity. He refused to back away, and took the same approach that won the fans' admiration after Yankees' pitcher Goose Gossage almost fractured his skull with a fastball in the 1981 World Series. Despite dizziness and double vision, the Penguin, a tough bird, was back in the lineup the next day. He singled the first time up and batted in the game-winning run before leaving.

"I came within a half-inch of being killed," Cey recalled of that instant, frozen in his memory, when Gossage's 95 m.p.h. bullet crashed into his head, splitting the plastic batting helmet. "My life was at stake.

Powerhouse Penguin led the Cubs in RBI.

Cey flashes his good glove in pursuit of a grounder headed for the hole.

"When situations come up now, they don't seem so bad."

Again, the Penguin didn't just fold his flippers in '83 when two errors cost the Cubs a game in his first week. Neither did he put his bat back in the rack, despite a .198 average after 24 games. The veteran also declined an opportunity to sit on the bench and feel sorry for himself after injuring his left shoulder May 24 in Houston. The sore muscle made it difficult to dive for grounders and it hurt when he swung the bat, but he played every day, offering no excuses.

Gradually, his persistence paid off. The familiar numbers came back when the struggling 1983 season wound down—24 homers, 90 RBI, .275 average. "I felt better about myself when it was over," Cey said.

From the standpoint of early frustration, 1984 started out like an instant replay. Injuries were up, batting average and morale down. Cey's left hand was banged up by a pitch June 23 and he strained ligaments in his right hand July 17. What hurt almost as much as a .212 mark at the plate.

"Some pitches, I just couldn't reach, because my top [right] hand wasn't strong enough," said Cey, who played down the stretch with both swollen wrists heavily bandaged. "I don't like alibis, but every ball I hit hard seemed to go right at somebody. Other guys were getting their share of bloop hits, and I wasn't. I started to wonder when they would fall in for me."

Cey finally hit on the right solution, hitting the ball where nobody could catch it. Suddenly, the Penguin was a vulture at the dish, devouring pitchers' mistakes for homers that won big games for the Cubs. He started a crucial east coast trip with a three-run blast July 23 in Philadelphia, bringing the Cubs from behind and giving them the momentum they needed to break the Eastern Division race wide open.

From then on, Cey transferred the pain he felt in the matched set of throbbing wrists, unloading most of it on opposing pitchers. The steel-nerved veteran learned long ago in Los Angeles how to respond when the heat's on, and he helped the Cubs stay in the race this year by employing Penguin Power.

"I wasn't ready to call it quits, just because things didn't happen right away," Cey pointed out. "When my average got down that low, all I did was start over."

BOWA TAKES A BOW

Coming through in September also was a reflex action for shortstop Larry Bowa, Cey's partner on the left side of the infield. The Cubs' captain was rested frequently midway through the season. But when every game became crucial, general manager Dallas Green made it clear who belonged in the starting lineup.

Green and manager Jim Frey were willing to give up some hitting in exchange for defensive stability at shortstop, especially with thunder in other Cub bats. Since Green and Bowa had been through a take-no-prisoners season, playoff, and World Series, when the Phillies went all the way in 1980, the Cub boss knew that his 5'10" shortstop had a 10'5" heart.

"I kept telling Frey, when it's all said and done, Bowa's gonna be playing," Green related. "Larry needs some confidence building, a feeling that Frey is counting on him. When the season turns into a dogfight, Bowa's at his best.

"He's not the greatest shortstop in the world anymore, but as long as Larry Bowa holds the Cub infield together and does things we know he's

Larry Bowa: Scrappy Captain.

"When I explain the situation to Larry, he rants and raves," Frey said. "He can't accept being 38, but until he gives us some pop at the plate, other guys will get a chance."

Kicking and screaming come naturally to Bowa, a compact, sturdy model of the work ethic. Above all else, he wants to win. The "play-me-or-trade-me" outburst, as Bowa acknowledged during his weekly talk show at a northwest suburban restaurant, was mainly a way of venting his frustration at not contributing more to the Cub charge.

"Offensively, I've let the team down," he said.

Wearing new glasses, Bowa gives the plate umpire a skeptical look after a close pitch.

capable of in tough situations, he'll play."

Bowa freely admits he's not easy to live with when Frey, or any manager, nails him to the bench. After winding up May with a stretch of five errors in five games, the captain got an unwelcome vacation, though Frey diplomatically pointed to a painfully jammed finger as the reason. Switch hitter Bowa continued to struggle from the left side; though he was as tough as ever to strike out, he wasn't making solid contact with pitches. For awhile, he wore glasses in a bid to snap out of the slump.

When it dragged on, Frey turned to veteran Tom Veryzer and rookie Dave Owen at short. Neither man was spectacular, and Green confessed that the position was near the top of his priority list with Bowa close to the end of a distinguished 15-year career. Bowa, incapable of giving in, thumbed his nose at the inevitable and vowed to play another year. He even asked to be traded or released, in the hope of catching on with another contender.

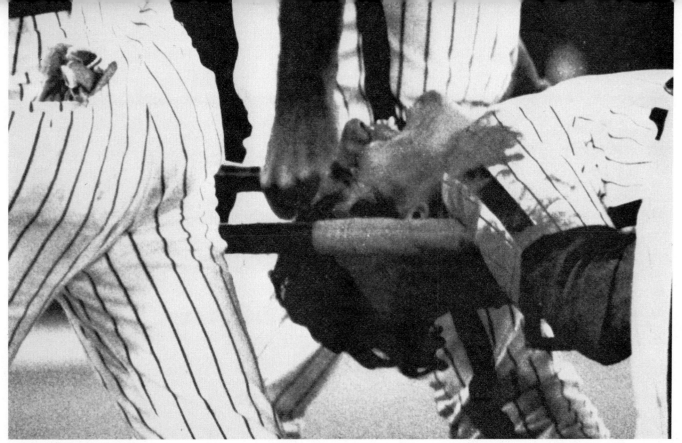

Larry Bowa's Philly teammates carry him off the field after the shortstop broke his leg attempting to steal.

Met Mookie Wilson can't stop Bowa from doubling up Danny Heep at first base.

**Bowa seems to be losing this duel of decibels with umpire John McSherry.
Manager Lee Elia (4) tries to keep peace.**

"Defensively, I've played well after a stretch of 12 errors in a month and a half. But the way Frey manages, everybody on the bench is there for a purpose. I'm anxious to do something to help, because when a team finishes fifth, you don't expect it to go all the way up next season."

After two years of watching young teammates make costly mistakes, Bowa was ready for 1984. He didn't want to leave the Cubs, or go anywhere except his familiar position every game.

"I've been in pennant races before, so I can relate to what's happening here," said Bowa, who came from Philadelphia in the fabulous 1982 trade that brought Ryne Sandberg to the Cubs. "When things happen the way they have for us, the feeling begins to grow in the clubhouse that it's your year. I saw it happen to the Phillies in 1980, when somebody would get the two-out hit to keep an inning alive or the umpire called a close 3-2 pitch the right way.

"I thought of that the other day, when Jody Davis scored two runs with a checked-swing hit," Bowa reflected. "Then Pete Rose's liner bounced off Lee Smith [August 2 in Wrigley Field], up in the air, and it's a double play. The Cubs really started believing it was their year when that happened."

Bowa detected light at the end of the tunnel while Cub fans were seeing only another late fadeout to bury the midseason optimism that lured some big crowds in 1983.

"I'm convinced we started to turn it then, even though it wasn't a great year," he said. "The Davises, Durhams, and Sandbergs put parts of their game together. They did good for awhile, then bad for awhile, but the young players came out of it figuring this club had ability. Once you erase the doubt about that, it changes from 'Maybe we can win' to 'I know we can win.' Last year, we had maybe 12 or 15 guys who believed. Go around the Cubs' clubhouse now and you'll find 25 guys believing."

Bowa became a big winner at home even before the Cubs followed suit on the field. He and his wife, Sheena, had their first child, daughter Victoria, in June, 1983, and she enabled him to put victories and defeats in perspective.

"The baby brought my wife and I closer together," Bowa said. "It made me realize what's really important in life."

Another Cub double play, as Cap'n Bowa nails Padre Graig Nettles and fires to first.

7

"JO-DEE! JO-DEE! JO-DEE!"

There's more than one "new tradition" at Wrigley Field nowadays. Ask Jody Davis about the fans' rhythmic chant of "Jo-dee! Jo-dee! Jo-dee!" and he'll tell you how good it makes him feel.

But when broadcasters, sportswriters, or other excitable types talk about "a life-or-death situation" in a baseball game, Davis just smiles that soft, Southern smile.

The Cubs' catcher has a very good reason for appreciating his life at the top. He has beaten higher odds than the standard 1,000-to-one against an unknown prospect like him becoming a National League All-Star. When the wheel of fortune spun for Davis in 1980, it really was a matter of life or death.

The lanky kid from the Georgia pines made steady progress through the bush leagues for four years, so the St. Louis Cards brought him to their St. Petersburg, Florida, training camp that spring. He was ticketed for one more year's polishing with the Cards' Springfield, Illinois, farm club and then a shot at the big time.

"I was their fifth catcher, behind Ted Simmons, Darrell Porter, Terry Kennedy, and Steve Swisher," Davis recalled. "That was all right, because I was moving up, even with a lot still to learn about the mechanics of catching."

Instead, Davis learned how fast a dream can turn into a nightmare. He reeled into the clubhouse one

Jody Davis: Georgia Plum.

Bull Durham heads the reception committee for Davis's homer.

The ball gets to Davis, but it's too late to prevent the Giants' Dusty Baker from scoring.

afternoon and began vomiting blood into a garbage can. Ken Reitz, then the Cards' third baseman and later a Cub teammate of Davis, will never forget the sight.

"I saw this big guy coughing up dried blood and then a lot of the fresh, red stuff," Reitz said. "After I helped the medics load him on a stretcher, I figured that's the last I'll see of him."

Reitz came close to being dead right. One operation failed to uncover the real problem, an abnormal artery in Davis's intestine, so emergency surgery was needed to save his life. Surgeons had to pump 31 pints of blood into the 23-year-old catcher to pull him through.

"After the first operation, when they just figured it was a stomach ulcer, I started throwing up blood again right away," Davis said. "I was too woozy to know if I would live or die, but as soon as they sewed up the leaky artery, everything was fine. Then it was only a matter of recuperating."

Not a bad attitude for such a close brush with death. Davis's reaction to that ordeal explains how he evolved into one of baseball's best catchers. Instead of whining about a bad break or brooding over the lost season, the soft-spoken redhead cheerfully played the hand fate had dealt him.

He went back home to Gainesville, Georgia, waiting impatiently until enough strength and weight had been regained to start working out. It didn't happen overnight, because Davis had lost 40 pounds off his splintery, 6'3", 200-pound frame. "At first, even jogging was too tough," he recalled. "All I could do was walk."

JODY CATCHES ON

Once his body could handle it, Jody got his career back on the right track, preparing for a long stay in the majors. With a grim note of irony, the Cards sent him back to their class A farm club in St. Petersburg, making him begin over in the same place where the end had almost been written.

Davis took advantage of the new lease on life, advancing to triple A in a few months, but the St. Louis brass figured the hard-luck kid wouldn't be able to make it all the way. They failed to protect him in the minor-league draft, so the Cubs grabbed the untried catcher for the $25,000 waiver price on December 8, 1980.

In another neat ironical touch, the Chicago general manager who snapped up that bargain was Bob Kennedy, whose son Terry had been scrambling, along with Davis, to stick with the Cards in that eventful spring of 1980.

Neither youngster suspected that in just four years, they would be ranked with the best at their position. How could they know that they would be vying for the NL pennant in 1984, with Davis behind the plate for the Cubs and Kennedy in the same spot for the San Diego Padres?

Before that could happen, Davis had to hurdle other obstacles in his path to stardom. In his first Cubs camp, the rookie was strictly a question mark, picked up on the notion that he might be adequate insurance for experienced receivers Barry Foote and Tim Blackwell. Instead, clubhouse lawyer Foote was traded to the Yankees early in the 1981 season and Davis took over the starting job from Blackwell in June. A .389 batting spree the previous month had removed all doubts about his hitting, but he still left something to be desired on defense.

Aware of the criticism, Davis worked on his faults, even though the payoff didn't come quickly. For a brief spell in 1982, he was shoved back to second-string status by a Philadelphia newcomer named Keith Moreland. Other Cubs assumed it was because general manager Dallas Green ordered the move, but Davis refused to pout. The result was a close friendship between the easygoing

Astro Bill Doran pays the price for trying to score on an infield grounder. Ron Cey's throw to Davis gets there first.

Georgian and Moreland, one that endured after each had found his proper niche in the Cub renaissance.

Even though Jody was still the number 1 Cub catcher after surviving Moreland's challenge, statistics continued to underline mechanical flaws in his technique. The time lapse from there to frenzied "Jo-dee!" bellows from Wrigley Field bleacherites was only 1½ seasons, but it was a bumpy trip.

Davis caught 150 games in 1983, although his performance behind the plate dipped sharply from the previous season's encouraging marks. He was charged with 21 passed balls, highest total in the league. Even more ominous was a soaring 74 percent success rate for baserunners attempting to steal on the Cub catcher, up from 59 percent in 1982. Those figures led to the dismissal of bullpen coach Duffy Dyer, but Davis refused to pin the blame on his teacher.

"I lost my confidence last year," Davis admitted during the 1984 season. "I wasn't making very good throws and it seemed like I couldn't throw anybody out."

At bat in 1983 the progress chart was considerably brighter. The slender right-handed swinger sparkled with a .271 average, 84 RBI, and an eye-popping 23 homers, doubling the previous season's bag.

"I always thought I could hit home runs, even back in high school and American Legion," Davis said. "My swing is tailored for driving the ball and I lift weights in the winter to increase my strength. In the last few years, I can tell it makes a difference in some extra pop at bat."

DIXIE COUP

Cub fans noticed as well; because they're used to whooping it up for Dixie dudes wearing catchers' gear. Randy Hundley, "the Rebel" of the 1969 pennant charge that failed, was a certified hero to the left-field Bleacher Bums in the era of manager Leo Durocher. From the moment Davis walked into the Cubs' clubhouse, he inherited the same good-guy label. His carrot-topped mane, down-home personality, and friendly smile were passports to a warm Chicago welcome. Even though Davis obviously lacked fellow Georgian Ty Cobb's ferocious temper, Wrigley Field Fans regarded him as another Georgia Peach.

So it wasn't a surprise when the "Jo-dee!" ritual

sprang up, seemingly by spontaneous combustion, during his 1983 home run spree against the Cards before overflow weekend crowds on June 10–12. Adding to the first stages of Cub Fever was the team's midseason fling at impersonating NL East contenders before fading to fifth place with a final 71–91 log for the 1983 season. When the Cubs made it clear early in '84 that they were in the race to stay, the chant for Jody became as much a tradition as Harry Caray's seventh-inning warbling.

"When you go out and hear those Cub rooters pulling for you every day, it's a great feeling," Davis said. "For some reason, the people in Chicago have been real good to me, even when my career wasn't going so well."

Stepping up to bat with runners on base is tough enough. Does the "Jo-dee!" uproar inspire him to swing for the seats?

"I don't think so," he replied. "Fans come to Wrigley Field to see the Cubs score runs and win. When I come up in a situation where we need a hit, I can't feel any more pressure because they're hollering encouragement at me. I hear them, but when it comes down to picking my pitch and hitting the ball, that's between me and the pitcher."

BACK TO BASICS

Davis clouted the horsehide often enough and far enough to carry a full share of the load while the 1984 Cubs amazed the baseball world by rocketing to the top of their division. Dallas Green and Jim Frey weren't concerned about that when the Cubs assembled for spring training in Mesa, Arizona. They were worried about the alarming skid in Davis' catching fundamentals during 1983. "Those [passed ball] totals have to be improved," cautioned Frey at the time, charitably refraining from adding that Davis had gunned down only 43 of 123 would-be base thieves.

Green scoffed at Davis's notion that his concentration had been affected by the "mental and physical drag" of catching in all except 11 of the 162-game season slate. "Baloney," Green barked. "That's a cop-out. If Jody isn't careful, he'll be labeled a part-time catcher."

The Cubs had no intention of letting that happen to anyone with Davis's blend of youth, talent, and potential. They hired Johnny Oates, a respected defensive catcher and Virginia gentleman, to succeed

Genial Jody throws a rare tantrum after plate umpire Steve Rippley called a third strike. Captain Larry Bowa tries to cool off his catcher.

As the fans cheer for "Jo-dee," the All-Star catcher slams another one out of the park.

Before the Cubs broke camp, the coach had chopped a half-second off Davis's clocking by teaching him to throw from a crouch.

"Jody's so tall and lanky that he loses time by standing up," Oates pointed out. "I told him not to worry about throwing the ball away. The main thing is, a catcher can't be tentative. He has to play aggressive defense."

That also carried over to calling pitches and taking responsibility for making Cub pitchers keep their concentration, two areas that Davis hadn't mastered. He was disturbed in previous seasons by manager Lee Elia's tendency to second guess his judgment in calling pitches.

"When batters got hits in those situations, I was blamed," Davis complained. "Nobody can stop major-league hitters every time. Now we have a pregame meeting to decide on a game plan for the starting pitcher. We stick with it, unless some of his pitches aren't working or his control isn't sharp. In that case, I'll go out to the mound and see if we can agree on something better."

Rapport between the Cubs' catcher and Oates soon wiped out the old your-guess-is-as-good-as-mine approach to handling pitchers. It was replaced by better mechanics, a take-charge attitude and quick success for Davis in preventing enemy runners from stealing him dizzy.

"The first thing Johnny told me was, 'Let's return to basics, have some fun, and see where we can go from there,' " Davis related. "It really has worked. I have much better communication with the pitchers and they have more confidence with me. They also like the way we've cut down on successful steals.

"Good baserunners will always get their share of stolen bases, but it looks like the word is getting around the league that they can't run at will anymore."

Dyer as bullpen coach. Oates's main mission, everyone knew, was to mold Davis into a better defensive catcher and stronger handler of pitchers. "Jody and I just need to talk things over and review his whole approach to these things," Oates began, pouring soothing syrup on ruffled feelings. "I guarantee he won't have 21 passed balls this season, even if he catches blindfolded."

From watching Cub games videotaped over the summer by his dad in Atlanta, Davis already had an idea how to correct that. He agreed with Oates that a tendency to be a passive receiver, without properly shifting his feet for pitches, led to the ones that got away.

So one solution came quickly, but that was only the beginning. Oates used a stopwatch to pinpoint seconds elapsed between the pitcher's release and arrival of the catcher's throw at second base.

"NEW" DAVIS A KEY PLAYER

The Cub staff agreed that the "new" Davis was a first-rate catcher. Just ask Steve Trout, who also came into his own this season. Trout made it clear that he wanted Davis behind the plate when he pitched. "I have to give Jody credit for my good start," Trout said. "When I get excited out there, he calms me down."

Bullpen bulwark Lee Smith added a pinch of

Jody Davis comes home to Bull Durham's greeting after a blast into the bleachers. Ron Cey waits his turn.

The Padres' Alan Wiggins uses Davis as a launching strip after forcing him at second base on the front end of a double play.

wry to his compliment: "Jody knows me better than I know myself," Smith said. "Sometimes that makes me feel a little sorry for him."

More important, Davis regained his confidence. His increased defensive value meant full-time duty wearing the so-called "tools of ignorance," but he became, in Frey's phrase, "the man we need back there." That key role was augmented by such consistent hitting that Davis was tapped to join second baseman Ryne Sandberg on the NL squad for the July 10 All-Star game in San Francisco.

Davis earned that recognition by bouncing back

from occasional miscues like the early-season passed ball that opened the gates for a 3–1 Cub loss in Houston. Davis made dramatic amends in the cavernous Astrodome the next day. Pinch hitting with two on and two out in the ninth inning, and his team down by a run, Davis slammed a 3–0 fastball from the Astros' Frank DiPino over the center-field wall for a game-breaking homer.

"I gave a game away last night, so I wanted to get one back for us," Davis said afterward. "Credit Jim Frey for giving me the green light on a 3–0 pitch."

A laid-back country boy, Davis is among the most popular Cubs because he prefers to let others take the bows. Even when things were not going well for the team, Davis usually could be relied on by the media not to disappear after a loss. He will sit by his locker on good days and bad, patiently explaining what happened in his quiet drawl.

That didn't change even when a troublesome midsummer slump had whittled close to fifty points from a robust .299 batting average at the All-Star break. He was frustrated, but spurned fatigue as an excuse, despite appearing in 119 of the Cubs' first 125 games. And when Jody temporarily broke out of it with a bang against those same Astros on August 21 in Wrigley Field, the self-needling sense of humor flashed again:

"About time," Davis said, with a mock sigh of relief. "They were starting to call me a defensive catcher."

No chance of that, since Davis was en route to the first over-100 RBI total by a Cub catcher since 1930, when Gabby Hartnett drove 122 across the plate. The realization that he was contributing heavily on defense increased his patience during the dry spell.

"If I can pull a pitcher through a tough game or throw a runner out, not hitting doesn't matter so much," Davis conceded. "But I like to swing the bat, too, so it gets old after awhile."

Still, Jody Davis is too modest to dwell on his talent. That's why he had been genuinely surprised when the New York Mets made him their third-round draft choice in the 1976 free agent baseball draft. The former basketball star at Oakwood, Georgia, High School figured his future was in that sport, so he enrolled at Middle Georgia College. "A friend of mine read my name in the Sporting News list of players who'd been drafted and called me," he said. "I couldn't believe it."

As an outfielder or infielder from a small town, Davis probably would have been overlooked by big-league ivory hunters. His height and strong throwing arm induced the Mets to make an offer, because good, big catching prospects are worth a gamble. They didn't know that the position was brand new to Davis.

"I had never caught in my life," he said. "Always played first base or outfield until my last year of American Legion ball. When our catcher got hurt, the manager asked if anybody else could catch and I told him, 'Heck, I'll try it.' "

It was a heck of a good decision.

Both benches explode into a gigantic Wrigley Field pileup after Keith Moreland charges the mound to let Mets pitcher Ed Lynch know that Cubs don't like to be targets. Both teams flail around while Jody Davis tries to find his pal Moreland under all those bodies.

8
ZONK AND DEER ENLIST IN SARGE'S BLEACHER ARMY

The Sarge has a busy schedule from reveille to taps. He's the Cubs' morale officer, inspector general of the Wrigley Field bleacher brigade, and designated clubhouse spokesman for visiting media. In between all those duties, Gary "Sarge" Matthews plays left field for the Cubs. And as his army in the left field bleachers knows, this 13-year veteran of the National League knows how to win wars.

KEEPING THE RANKS IN LINE

Long before hand-to-hand combat for the NL East title got serious, the Sarge was putting Cub recruits through basic training. Center fielder Bob Dernier, who came from Philadelphia with Matthews in a March 27 trade, credits his outfield buddy with helping him make the adjustment to regular status. Matthews aided Leon Durham and other youngsters that way, also not hesitating to motion Cub veterans aside for a word about their attitude.

"If people think I've had a leadership role on this team, well and good," Matthews shrugged off his dugout diplomacy. "I think I'm part of why the Cubs are winning, because I have a winning attitude. The thing that really made the difference was

Gary Matthews: Sarge sizzles.

They can't all land in the bleachers. Matthews popped this pitch up, but later delivered still another game-winning hit.

Sarge salutes Mel Hall's game-winning single against Pittsburgh.

25 guys knowing they all have a part to play, so a Ryne Sandberg or a Lee Smith don't have to do it every day."

Matthews did much more than keep the Cubs fired up all season, and he decided to take personal charge down the stretch. He lifted the lid on September with a clutch ninth-inning double in a nationally televised game against Atlanta, the Sarge's 14th game-winning hit.

Sarge was in line for promotion to top kick when he did it again two days later. This time, he showed the Phillies what a blunder unloading him had been by snuffing out their faint hopes for a successful NL East defense. He put on a show for Philadelphia fans, homering off Steve Carlton, then driving across the winning run in the 12th inning.

"Whatever it takes to win," Matthews stressed. "We're all in this together."

True, although some have bigger roles than others. The veteran has been a star from the start, contributing to the Cubs' pregame confidence level, as well as on the field. General manager Dallas Green believes enlisting the Sarge shook the Cubs out of their springtime lethargy.

"Matthews expresses emotion," Green pointed out. "Looking at our club early on, we didn't have the guys who did that. Some were leaders in their own sense, but not the emotional kind.

"Every now and then, it's not too bad to have one of those around. That's what the Pete Rose-style sliding on your belly is all about. It stirs things up, gets people moving."

Matthews knows how to do that. Besides getting the game-breaking hit more often than any other Cub, he led the team in walks and on-base percentage, and kept the fans entertained with acrobatic catches in left field.

When the Cubs were still taking close-order drill in the opening month, the Sarge didn't hesitate to pull rank. Angered when manager Jim Frey benched him April 26 to give Mel Hall a start in left, the veteran grumbled, "I don't know why Frey did that to me." Frey merely kept on making the moves he felt necessary, so Sarge quickly decided to remain a good soldier. Once Bill Buckner, another would-be rival for the left-field slot, was shipped to Boston May 25 in a swap for pitcher Dennis Eckersley, Matthews could relax and enjoy himself. He made sure Cub fans had fun, too.

Matthews leads the team in walks, but here he gets a pitch he can slam.

"I went through two stretches of being benched in my career, so I know how Buckner felt," he said. "I figured when I came over here the Cubs had a clue on offense, so getting pitchers like Eck and the Red Baron [Rick Sutcliffe] during the season filled in the missing pieces.

"Before this season, nobody took the Cubs seriously. When we were swept by Philly [a four-game Wrigley Field disaster in June], most of the fans thought, 'Well, here they go again, same old Cubs.' Even friends of mine on the Phillies told me they didn't think we could bounce back. I told 'em we'd be heard from."

The label of free swinger had been pinned on Matthews ever since 1973, when he was a rookie on the San Francisco Giants. His power caused fans to overlook a selective eye that earned an above-average total of bases on balls. So when Matthews cropped up as Cub leader in walks, even he was a little startled. The explanation was simple enough. Frequently batting with the Daily Double, Bob Dernier and Ryne Sandberg, on base ahead of him, the Sarge was worked on very carefully, enabling his on-base percentage to top theirs.

"Sometimes they pitch to me and sometimes they don't," he said of the free passes that kept turning into Cub runs. 'When I get on, the guys up next have been taking advantage. A bunch of them are bringing me around. It's a compliment that pitchers don't take me for granted." Very few

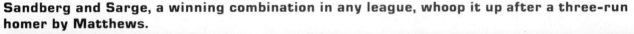

Sandberg and Sarge, a winning combination in any league, whoop it up after a three-run homer by Matthews.

people, including pitchers, reacted to the Sarge with indifference this season. He proved formidable with a bat, glove, or just a big grin for his left-field bleacher army.

The daily routine of smiles, waves, and small talk evolved into a between-innings exchange of salutes between Sarge and his troops. After decades of frustration, the Wrigley bleachers finally became more than a tanning spa and open-air beer garden. Way back in 1969, the Bleacher Bums wore hard hats, responded to cheers led by bullpen eccentric Dick Selma, and sang oldies but goodies—"Gimme that Old-Time Durocher" and "You Gotta Stop Kickin' My Dog Around."

With Matthews as the catalyst, that kind of sideshow made a comeback. The difference was that the 1984 Cubs were a better team, and they didn't fold in the stretch. "These fans let me know what they think," the Sarge said. "They've given the whole team a lift, not just me."

In reciprocation, Matthews handed out caps decorated with sergeant's stripes, only to find himself topped the following week. Before the Cubs ended a homestand against the Reds August 29,

Keith Moreland: The Zonk factor.

bleacherites got 3,500 T-shirts reading "It's a Blast in the Bleachers—Zonk, Deer, J.D., Bull, and Ryno." Such largesse produced an $8,000 tab for Keith "Zonk" Moreland, "Deer" Dernier, Jody "J.D." Davis, Leon "Bull" Durham, and "Ryno" Sandberg. They figured it was a good investment.

ZONK RISES TO ANY OCCASION

Moreland wasn't used to such accolades, at least not until this season. For two years, bleacher fans had been skeptical of his fielding, but now they rose only to rave about the way he kept rising to the occasion with runners on base. Constant struggle had taught Moreland how to cope with Wrigley Field's nightmarish afternoon pattern of sun, shadows, and sneaky wind, but in training camp this spring, he didn't feel secure. Trade rumors had dogged him all winter.

An earnest, honest worker, the ex-University of Texas defensive back picked up his nickname in Philadelphia: "Zonker" for a "Doonesbury" cartoon character. He also brought a good-hit, no-field reputation to Chicago on December 8, 1981, when the Phillies traded him, with pitchers Dickie Noles and Dan Larson, for pitcher Mike Krukow.

Moreland became an adequate fielder, and his versatility was an asset. He had brief stints at catcher and third base, plus occasional chores at first base. Whenever—and whatever—he played, there was no doubt about Moreland's ability to hit major league pitching.

But the easygoing Texan was so frustrated that he startled teammates by singing "Please Release Me" on the plane to San Francisco for the 1984 season opener. He was aware that Dallas Green had tried—and failed—to deal him to four other clubs. Moreland grew unhappier when it became clear that manager Jim Frey intended to platoon him in right field with Mel Hall.

"The Cubs need a left-handed relief pitcher," Moreland said. "Why not trade me to get one? I'm not happy, but they know that won't stop me from playing hard."

Green and Frey were aware of that. Moreland had just avoided salary arbitration, signing a two-year contract worth more than $1 million. Unlike many players who would be overjoyed to sit on that bundle, he can't be content as a spectator.

"This spring, Zonk was terrible, just like a lot of

The Phillies used Moreland behind the plate—a tough way to make a living.

Keith Moreland comes out of the Cubs' dugout to salute fans for their ovations after his grand slam, which provided all the runs in a 4-3 triumph.

people I was counting on to contribute," Green recalled. "He can get in the Mike Schmidt cool thing pretty quick when he's comfortable, and that's how he felt after [a .302 average] last season. There was some heavy pouting when we made the Dernier and Matthews trade and sat Zonk's butt down for awhile, but I knew all along he would contribute. It was just a matter of when and where Frey would need him to get it done.

"When he came to us, Jimmy [Frey] wasn't a Zonk fan," the general manager noted. "He was seeing only what he saw of him in spring training, which wasn't too pretty. I told him, 'Jimmy, the guy loves RBI situations, loves to put this pressure on himself. He'll be fine.' Frey saw it happen after we traded Mel Hall to Cleveland."

So did everybody else. Along with bringing phenomenal Rick Sutcliffe to the Cubs, that June 13 deal with the Indians turned right field into Moreland's personal patch of turf. He responded with a batting spree that propelled baseballs over fences and the Cubs into first place.

Suddenly the sign reading "How would the manager like to be platooned?" disappeared from

Moreland plunges into Wrigley Field vines in vain pursuit of a triple by Houston's Dickie Thon. The rightfielder won't give up on anything hit his way.

Full extension shows Moreland making solid contact with this pitch. Torrid August locked up NL Player of the Month laurels for Zonk.

Moreland's locker. It was replaced by a daily media mob, asking about the Cub slugger's latest heroics—and there were plenty. In 43 games of spot duty before the Hall trade, Moreland batted a mediocre .237, with only two home runs and 11 RBI. When he became a regular, Zonk smoked the ball at a .321 clip over the next 65 games, clouting a dozen homers and driving in 54 runs. When Sutcliffe (6–0, 3.52 ERA) became an easy choice for top NL pitcher in August, Moreland gave the Cubs a sweep of the August honors by being named NL Player of the Month, batting .360, with five home runs and 32 RBI.

"Playing every day and helping the Cubs into first place," Moreland said with a beatific smile. "This is what I've always wanted. The Cubs don't have to be spoilers and play for personal pride anymore. Now it's team pride."

Moreland was a one-man team during an incred-

ible first week of August, when the Cubs took command of the NL East race. He put on a Wrigley Field show that ranked with the fence-busting exploits of Billy Williams when the Sweet Swinger was in one of his hot streaks. In a pack of eight critical games from August 1 through 7, Moreland sparked the Cubs to a 7–1 blitz by coming to bat 30 times and rapping 15 hits, four of them homers, for a .500 clip. Collecting 11 RBI and at least as many pitchers' scalps along the way, Zonk capped the spree with three game-winning hits.

Then he charged the mound after the Mets' Ed Lynch clipped him on the hip with a pitch August 7, just to let New York and the rest of the baseball universe know the Cubs could not be intimidated.

"I have no hard feelings for Lynch," Moreland said. "If he had aimed at my head, it would have been a different story."

If one of those aborted Moreland trades had

In his earlier days with the Cubs, Moreland preferred the shaggy look. Now he's cleaner-shaven, leaner, and meaner at the plate.

gone through, the Cubs might well be saying the same thing about their triumphal season.

NOTHING RUNS LIKE A DEER

While Zonk and Sarge swung the heavy lumber, Bob Dernier was supposed to handle the glove work in the Cubs' outfield. The fleet center fielder lived up to advance billing in the power alleys and on the basepaths, leading the club in clutch catches and stolen bases. His prowess in both departments was no upset. The Phillies gave up on "Deer," including him in the Matthews trade only because they figured he could not hit big-league pitching consistently.

Green would have been satisfied with just Dernier's glove and speed. He wanted a center fielder in the worst way, which is how the Cubs had been getting them for years. It was a pleasant surprise to find the new glove man batting well over .300 until after the All-Star break, when his average tailed off.

"Getting Dernier was really the key," Green said. "It set our outfield. We never had a center fielder or a leadoff man here in God knows how many years. All those experiments with Mel Hall, Larry Bowa,

or Ryne Sandberg in the leadoff spot didn't work. Sandberg does too many things too well to bat first. I knew Dernier would anchor the defense and let us play the speed game, with Sandberg hitting second and playing second base, where he performs best.

"The Sutcliffe trade was great, especially for that time of the year," Green pointed out. "But for me, the thing that got it started was Matthews and Dernier. By the time Sutcliffe and the rest of those guys got here, we could have been in last place. Matthews and Dernier got us juiced, and it sent a message to the ballclub: 'Hey, guys, we ain't fooling around here. If you don't pay attention to the job, we're gonna get people who do.' "

Dernier did it from the day he showed up. He proved that 82 stolen bases over the two previous seasons was no fluke, joining Sandberg in a stampede on the base paths that transformed the Cubs' stodgy, stand-pat image into one of speed and daring.

"The Cubs gave me a chance because of my speed," Dernier admitted. "I'll give them some results. Making big plays, running down a long drive and catching it really gives me a kick."

Bob Dernier: Man in Motion.

**Bob Dernier tiptoes safely home on Gary Matthews's sacrifice fly.
The Giants' catcher Steve Nicosia stabs the late throw.**

Dernier clings to the bag, waiting for the bad news on this rare occasion, when he was nabbed trying to stretch a single to left. San Francisco's Brad Wellman recovers his balance after making the tag.

Dernier swiftly began collecting both kicks and baseballs, staging a daily outfield clinic for bug-eyed Wrigley Field spectators. He was even better in the left-center and right-center gaps on the NL's artificial rugs in St. Louis, Philadelphia, Pittsburgh, Cincinnati, Montreal, and Houston, robbing batters of extra-base hits in parks that had been Cub burial grounds.

The burglary that summed up Dernier's value came during a close one on July 6 in San Francisco. The Cubs and struggling relief ace Lee Smith thought the game against the Giants was over, when Wohlford hit an easy grounder. Unfortunately, it was ruled a foul ball, so the Cardiac Cubs had to play it again.

Given new life, Wohlford almost killed the Cubs with a blast to right center, ticketed to bring home the winning run. Dernier brought his team back to life with an even better jump than usual, making a sensational grab at full gallop.

"He makes those kinds of catches, the ones other center fielders don't get close to," conceded Phillies' scout Hugh Alexander.

So how come they gave up on him?

"I wondered about that myself," Dernier said. "It was so discouraging, I began to think maybe baseball was not for me. People told me I should have complained about the way the Phillies treated me. I kept quiet because I was a rookie, but I still don't know what they expected of me."

Cub fans certainly never expected Dernier to rank among the top 10 NL hitters at midseason. Encouraged by the news that Frey wasn't trying to convert the right-handed batter into a switch hitter (an experiment which failed in Philadelphia), Dernier became an all-around contributor. "I'm probably not a .320 hitter, but I can do better than .220," he said. "As long as I hit well enough to play regularly, that's fine. Helping us out with a good catch makes me tingle all over."

And with Dernier blanketing the outfield, Cub pitchers no longer are shaking all over.

"Deer" Dernier, the first half of the Cubs' Daily Double, is at it again for his 28th stolen base. He topped his previous major-league high of 42 before the Cubs clinched the NL East.

9
HOME FREE
WITH LEE AND
CUB SUPERSUBS

When he was a kid in Louisiana in Pistol Pete Maravich country, Lee Smith preferred to stuff the ball into a hoop instead of stuffing it down batters' throats. He was playing basketball, not baseball, in those days. A lot of National League batters think Smitty should have stuck with it.

When the Cubs' ace fireman is smoking them out nowadays, at 95 miles per hour or so, his pitches rocket past their bats like Halley's Comet. In those you-or-me spots, with a game on the line, the relievers who thrive and survive have big hearts and matching fast balls.

Ask most fans to name their top three in the bullpen and you get Bruce Sutter, St. Louis; Goose Gossage, San Diego; and Dan Quisenberry, Kansas City. Smith often is overlooked, a strange fate for somebody who's 6'6" and 235 pounds. It's even more frustrating, because Smith was the Cubs' only overpowering pitcher in his first four seasons. Now that the starters need less help, a series of nagging injuries has taken about 6 inches off his high, hard one.

"Lately, I haven't thrown many good fast balls," Smith lamented. "I've been concentrating on making good first pitches. Keeps me out of the hole."

Lee Smith: Fire Chief.

A contented circle of Cubs: Larry Bowa, Jody Davis, Lee Smith, Ron Cey, and Don Zimmer savor Smitty's save.

75

You can bet Smitty's not unleashing a change-up at this Atlanta batter.

A real bull session in Comiskey Park among **NL All-Stars Terry Kennedy, Lee Smith, and Leon "Bull" Durham.**

Rick Bordi: Surprise package.

But the hole he can't stay out of is on the Wrigley Field mound. A swollen left knee has hampered Smith's delivery, and he believes it's aggravated by pitching at home. "The drop-off is gradual, not straight down like St. Louis, so I have a tendency to step in other pitchers' holes," he said. "My pitches come in higher."

Despite aches and pains up and down his towering frame, Smith's numbers are healthy. He's racking up career highs in wins and saves this season, though an ERA well over his lifetime 2.53 indicates a velocity gap. The thought of it brings on one of those monumental Smith frowns, only slightly less intimidating than his heater.

"I'm not slacking off for injuries," he said. "Doesn't matter if I'm shooting marbles, man, I try to win. A pennant race is nice, but in late relief, all the incentive I need is me against the batter."

Smith showed he could win those duels even before settling into the bullpen, but the burly right-hander still had to be convinced he wasn't a starter. After just one start in his first two seasons, he started five more games in 1982, then accepted his fate. The decision sealed the fate of many rallies by Cub opponents. Before long, Smitty had inherited the bullpen throne abdicated in 1980 by King Sutter.

"I know that's where I belong," he said. "All I need is to be involved in the games. It's hard to get some ink when you're sitting."

CUBS STRIKE IT RICH

That wasn't a problem for Rich Bordi, who stopped waiting and began winning this season. When the Cubs gave him spot starts after some effective relief outings, Bordi made the most of them. The 6'7" right-hander stopped Houston 10–3 on May 20 for his first big-league victory. His inconsistency vanished under the magic touch of Cub pitching coach Billy Connors.

"I'm happier than a kid on his first bicycle," grinned Bordi, 0–2 in American League stints with Oakland and Seattle and 0–2 for the Cubs in 1983. He came over in the trade that sent outfielder Steve Henderson to the Mariners, and then shuttled between the Cubs and their Iowa farm. No ball of fire in either place, his sudden emergence was a bonus, both in relief and as a starter.

Bordi's nifty relief stint September 1 in Atlanta paid off with a 4–1 win, hiking his record to 5–1 and giving the Cubs momentum for their last long trip. He took over for Dennis Eckersley in the eighth inning, striking out Braves Albert Hall and Claudell Washington with sharp benders. It was encouraging proof of recovery from back spasms that had put him on the 15-day disabled list in August.

"Billy has me concentrating on staying ahead of the hitters," said Bordi, who walked only 19 in his first 72 innings.

BIG TIM'S BIG TIME

The third leg of the bullpen's tall trio is another ex-basketball player, 6'7" Tim Stoddard from North Carolina State. He teamed with All-American David Thompson, sparking the Wolfpack to a 57–1 record in two years, including victory over Bill Walton and UCLA, and the 1974 NCAA crown.

Despite his bulk, topped by a menacing mustache, Stoddard has learned how to relax, keeping the rest of the bullpen crew loose with one-liners. When he's summoned to the mound with the

Tim Stoddard: Big relief.

George Frazier: A helping right hand.

winning runs on base, it's a different matter.

"I don't go out there to trick people," Stoddard said. "They know I'm coming right at them with a fast ball and slider."

The formula worked like a charm earlier in the season, when Stoddard pitched well enough to alternate with Lee Smith in late-game situations. Then he developed control problems and manager Jim Frey began to look elsewhere in the bullpen.

LET GEORGE DO IT

Fortunately for the Cubs, the Rick Sutcliffe trade with Cleveland also deposited George Frazier on their doorstep. Frazier wasted no time proving he could hack it in the NL, fanning 5 of the 10 Phillies he faced in a June 14 mop-up job.

"I'm glad to be here," the right-hander said. "It doesn't matter to me who gets the decision or the save, as long as the Cubs win. My father taught me to be a team player, and I've been that way ever since high school."

RICK, BRU PLAY THEIR PART

With a well-stocked bullpen snapping up what-

ever crusts the Cub starters left lying around, there was little to do for Rick Reuschel and Warren Brusstar, two of the Cubs' veterans. Brusstar got in some effective relief work here and there, but Reuschel, in his second tour of duty with the team, lost a starting role after some good efforts were not backed up by the usual lusty offense. He went on the disabled list with mysterious back and shoulder problems in late August, enabling Bordi to rejoin the roster, and saw only limited action down the stretch.

Reuschel gave the Cubs a lift when they needed one by taming the Phillies 12–3 on June 2 in Philadelphia. It eased the sting of the previous night's wipeout, when some rare sloppy defense had handed the Phils seven unearned runs. That provided consolation for toughies like the 1–0 Astrodome loss pinned on sturdy right-hander Reuschel May 13, despite yielding just three hits in his first complete game since 1981. Though he was unhappy about spectator status, Reuschel approved the Cubs' new look.

"It may seem like some kind of miracle, but the Cubs really are winning with fundamental baseball," said the veteran, who had been shipped to

Rick Reuschel: Home again.

Warren Brusstar: Waiting his turn.

George Steinbrenner's Bronx Zoo in 1981, after a decade in Chicago. "In the past, a starter expected two or three runs to work with, at most. Now we're scoring, taking advantage of the breaks, and getting production from everybody.

"It's not like the Yankees, who won because they were expected to win," Reuschel noted. "They didn't play sound baseball, but their attitude covered up a lot of mistakes. I'd rather win the way the Cubs are doing it."

BENCH AND SPLINTER GROUP

A deeper bench was part of Frey's master plan, but Blue Cross rates shot up steeply this season among the Cubs' reserve corps. Ron Hassey, the catcher who came from Cleveland with Sutcliffe and Frazier, strained left knee ligaments July 4, depriving the Cubs of a left-handed hitting backup for overworked Jody Davis. The other reserve catcher, Steve Lake, had even worse luck, catching little else after he got hepatitis from tainted seafood on the first trip of the season.

Lake spent a month in the hospital, losing weight and strength while fighting the debilitating disease.

After Hassey got hurt, Lake was summoned from rehabilitation at his Phoenix home. He survived 10 days in searing heat with the Midland, Texas, farm club, slowly regaining playing form. "If Jody gets hurt, I'll be ready," Lake promised.

One of the biggest disappointments was the baffling shoulder malady that took Richie Hebner, the well-traveled spinner of clubhouse yarns, out of the picture as a productive lefty pinch hitter and utility infielder. Prolonged therapy and exercise didn't seem to help a condition diagnosed as tendinitis and aggravation of the rotator cuff.

The same bad luck, in the form of a broken thumb, put reserve shortstop Tom Veryzer on the shelf. Sent to Midland for some work after it healed, Veryzer went AWOL, but rejoined the Cubs in time to give them some backup shortstop. So did Dave Owen, the rookie summoned from Iowa to replace Veryzer, then sent back until the September 1 end to roster limits.

The battle for shortstop was a prime example of Frey's inclination to let players fight it out for supremacy at every position, with the hottest bats and gloves getting the starting nod. Neither Larry Bowa, Veryzer, nor Owen hit exceptionally well, though

Spruced up for Opening Day, Wrigley Field lures a full house to see Rick Reuschel toss the first pitch of 1981 to Met Mookie Wilson.

Steve Lake: Back in gear.

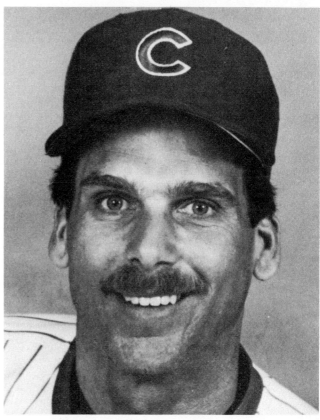

Richie Hebner: On the shelf.

Tom Veryzer: Steady and ready.

Dave Owen: Young and willing.

Bob Dernier congratulates Dave Owen for the rookie's pinch single. It wrapped up a colossal Cubs comeback with a 12-11 triumph over the Cards in 11 drama-packed innings.

all fielded acceptably, so Frey went with Bowa's experience until the NL East crown was in the vault. Reserve infielder Dan Rohn was used mainly as a lefty pinch hitter.

Despite the injury plague among the substitutes, there was enough outfield depth to release Jay Johnstone when Frey became convinced that the pinch hitter's bat no longer contained home-run power. That was tough, since J.J.'s pranks helped ease the pressure on everybody. The move reflected the true nature of the baseball business. It's hard

and unsentimental, despite all the surface glamor.

Deeply disappointed, Johnstone dropped his bat and grabbed a mike for Chicago's Channel 7. The garrulous guy was well-suited to the new job. He had attended Pete Rose's comeback press conference in Cincinnati to ask the 43-year-old Reds skipper, "Pete, when are you going to bring the designated hitter rule to the NL?" J.J. also was given unofficial coaching status "to ease the pain," in Dallas Green's words.

J.J. was dispensible because two other outfielders, Thad Bosley and Henry Cotto, displayed sensational bat and glove work, plus base-stealing speed, in backup roles. Bosley earned his 1984 salary with one swing, bringing the Cubs from behind with a dramatic ninth-inning homer August 30 in Atlanta. The blast off of the Braves' Gene Garber tied it at 3–3, and the aroused visitors broke the game open in the tenth. It was by no means Bosley's only clutch hit, merely another indication of the magic spell the Cubs wove in 1984.

"I'm finally starting to feel like I belong," said Bosley, a survivor at 28, after bouncing around to four AL teams and emerging as the only nonroster

Jay Johnstone: J.J. keeps 'em loose.

Thad Bosley, the unsung hero of the Cub turnabout, steals a base, one of his many talents. The Braves' Ken Oberkfell can't handle the throw.

Henry Cotto: Hit and run.

Cotto shows a happy crowd he still has the ball after a spectacular catch.

player to stick in training camp. "I've hit the ball and contributed on defense everywhere, but now I'm getting noticed. On a winning team, everything works better."

The supersub tandem of left-handed Bosley and right-handed Cotto certainly fit into that category. When center fielder Bob Dernier pulled a thigh muscle and had to miss a week of decision in early August, Cotto met the challenge head-on. He roamed the outfield, plucking potential extra-base hits out of the vines and shocking Phillies' slugger Mike Schmidt by throwing him out at second base on a drive off the left-field wall. The rookie also showed consistency at bat.

"Young players have to be ready all the time," said Cotto, who sent most of his salary home to his family in Puerto Rico. "You never know when the chance will come."

Still, it got crowded and frustrating in the waiting line, where Bosley and Cotto were joined by Gary Woods, a steady veteran with defensive ability, speed, and occasional power. The youngsters cut into his 1984 appearances. "Playing time hasn't worked out too well for me, but nobody wants to complain when the team is winning," Woods philosophized. "I'd rather stay with the Cubs and contribute what I can than go somewhere else for 75 or 100 more at-bats that didn't mean much."

Some other spare parts were summoned after the Iowa Cubs had been ousted by the White Sox's Denver farm in the American Association playoffs, but not the prize prospect, shortstop Shawon Dunston. In the scouts' opinion, Dunston was not yet ready for prime time. Rookie speedster Billy Hatcher pitched in right away with a vital stolen base. Owen returned as well, along with pitchers Reggie Patterson, Bill Johnson, and Ron Meredith.

So Dallas Green raked in one more chip from the pot, picking up 38-year-old Davey Lopes from Oakland to complete the trade that had sent pitcher Chuck Rainey to the A's. Despite aging legs and eye problems, Lopes, a former Dodger teammate of Ron Cey, had been through pennant and playoff pressure. He doubled on the first pitch thrown to him as a Cub, indicating that the old warhorse had a few furlongs left.

"Lopes protects us at third base, second base, and the outfield," Frey said. "He knows how to win, and you need those kind of people in the playoffs."

Playoffs? The Chicago Cubs? At long last, yes.

Gary Woods: Bench strength.

As the Dodgers' second baseman, Davey Lopes hurt his wrist trying to nail Jerry White of the Expos. As a Cub, Lopes's experience will come in handy during the playoffs.

Gary Woods floats through the air with the greatest of ease to rob Red Eddie Milner with a sensational catch.

APPENDIX
CHICAGO CUBS 1984 ROSTER

Pitchers

NO.	NAME	BATS/ THROWS	HEIGHT	WEIGHT	BIRTH DATE	RESIDENCE
42	Bordi, Rich	R/R	6'7"	220	4-18-59	San Francisco, CA
41	Brusstar, Warren	R/R	6'3"	200	2-2-52	Belmont Shores, CA
43	Eckersley, Dennis	R/R	6'2"	200	10-3-54	Wayland, MA
39	Frazier, George	R/R	6'5"	200	10-13-54	Tulsa, OK
36	Johnson, Bill[1]	R/R	6'5"	205	10-6-60	Wilmington, DE
52	Patterson, Reggie[1]	L/R	6'4"	185	11-7-58	Bessemer, AZ
38	Meredith, Ron[1]	L/L	6'0"	175	11-26-56	Ridgelands, CA
48	Reuschel, Rick	R/R	6'3"	225	5-16-49	Arlington Heights, IL
44	Ruthven, Dick	R/R	6'3"	190	3-27-51	Glen Mills, PA
24	Sanderson, Scott	R/R	6'5"	200	7-22-56	Northbrook, IL
46	Smith, Lee	R/R	6'6"	235	12-4-57	Castor, LA
49	Stoddard, Tim	R/R	6'7"	250	3-8-57	Timonium, MD
40	Sutcliffe, Rick	L/R	6'7"	225	6-21-56	Lee's Summit, MO
34	Trout, Steve	L/L	6'4"	190	7-30-57	Crete, IL

Catchers

NO.	NAME	BATS/ THROWS	HEIGHT	WEIGHT	BIRTH DATE	RESIDENCE
7	Davis, Jody	R/R	6'3"	210	11-12-56	Gainesville, GA
15	Hassey, Ron	L/R	6'2"	195	2-27-53	Tucson, AZ
16	Lake, Steve	R/R	6'1"	190	3-14-57	Inglewood, CA

Infielders

NO.	NAME	BATS/ THROWS	HEIGHT	WEIGHT	BIRTH DATE	RESIDENCE
1	Bowa, Larry[2]	S/R	5'10"	155	12-6-45	Seminole, FL
11	Cey, Ron	R/R	5'9"	185	2-15-48	Woodland Hills, CA
10	Durham, Leon	L/L	6'2"	210	7-31-57	Cincinnati, OH
18	Hebner, Richie	L/R	6'1"	200	11-26-47	Walpole, MA
12	Lopes, Davey	R/R	5'9"	170	5-3-46	Pacific Palisades, CA
19	Owen, Dave[1]	S/R	6'2"	170	4-25-58	Cleburne, TX
17	Rohn, Dan	L/R	5'7"	165	1-10-56	Alpena, MI
23	Sandberg, Ryne	R/R	6'2"	180	9-18-59	Tempe, AZ
29	Veryzer, Tom	R/R	6'1"	180	2-11-53	Islip, NY

Outfielders

NO.	NAME	BATS/ THROWS	HEIGHT	WEIGHT	BIRTH DATE	RESIDENCE
27	Bosley, Thad	L/L	6'3"	175	9-17-56	Oceanside, CA
28	Cotto, Henry	R/R	6'2"	180	1-5-61	Caguas, PR
20	Dernier, Bob	R/R	6'0"	160	1-5-57	Independence, MO
22	Hatcher, Billy[1]	R/R	5'9"	175	10-4-60	Williams, AZ
21	Johnstone, Jay[1]	L/R	6'1"	190	11-20-46	San Marino, CA
36	Matthews, Gary	R/R	6'3"	190	7-5-50	Wynnewood, PA
6	Moreland, Keith	R/R	6'0"	200	5-2-54	Dallas, TX
25	Woods, Gary	R/R	6'2"	190	7-20-53	Santa Barbara, CA

Manager: Jim Frey, 8   Trainer: Tony Garafolo

Coaches: Billy Connors, 3   Team Doctor: Jacob Suker, M.D.
             Johnny Oates, 9
             Ruben Amaro, 5
             John Vukovich, 2
             Don Zimmer, 4

[1]Not eligible for playoffs.   [2]Team captain.